Introduction to Microcomputers
and Microprocessors

Introduction to Microcomputers and Microprocessors

ARPAD BARNA

Hewlett-Packard Laboratories
Palo Alto, California

DAN I. PORAT

Stanford Linear Accelerator Center
Stanford University
Stanford, California

A WILEY-INTERSCIENCE PUBLICATION

JOHN WILEY & SONS, New York • London • Sydney • Toronto

Library of Congress Cataloging in Publication Data:

Barna, Arpad.
    Introduction to microcomputers and microprocessors.

    "A Wiley-Interscience publication."
    Bibliography: p.
    Includes index.
    1. Miniature computers. 2. Microprocessors.

I. Porat, Dan I., joint author. II. Title.
QA76.5.B293   001.6'4'04   75-31675
ISBN 0-471-05051-2

Printed in the United States of America

10 9 8 7 6 5 4

Preface

The introduction of an ever-increasing variety of microcomputers and microprocessors has led to a great diversity in their applications. The design of microprocessor-based systems, however, involves an understanding of several disciplines, including logic design, digital systems, computer architecture, programming, and to a lesser degree electronic circuit design and semiconductor technology. This introductory book is written for the beginner who does not have a detailed knowledge of these fields but who wants to learn the techniques required for the efficient use of microcomputers and microprocessors.

The subject is presented in three stages. The first three chapters provide an overview of the basic hardware and software, the next five chapters detail the operation, and the last chapter presents additional features. Each chapter can stand on its own, with a minimum of cross-referencing, so that the reader can omit chapters without impairing readability and can conveniently utilize the material for reference.

The 120 examples and problems incorporated in the text make the book particularly suited for self-study, providing a solid basis for understanding the characteristics of the wide variety of available microcomputers and microprocessors. The references listed at the end of the book provide additional material on the subjects discussed. Answers to selected problems are also given.

ARPAD BARNA
DAN I. PORAT

Stanford, California
September 1975

Contents

List of Abbreviations

ALU	arithmetic-logic unit
BCD	binary-coded decimal
ASCII	American Standard Code for Information Interchange
CCD	charge-coupled device
CPU	central processor unit
DMA	direct memory access
I/O	input-output
MAR	memory address register
MDR	memory data register
MOS	metal-oxide-silicon
MOSFET	metal-oxide-silicon field-effect transistor
PLA	programmable logic array
pROM	programmable read-only memory
RAM	random-access memory
ROM	read-only memory

Introduction to Microcomputers
and Microprocessors

1

Perspective

One of the most significant steps in the development of digital computers was the introduction of the *stored-program computer.** Unlike an abacus or manually operated desk calculator, the operating sequence in a stored-program computer is controlled by an internally stored *program.*

> **Example 1.1.** Vehicular traffic at the intersection of a principal and a secondary road is regulated by a traffic controller that has a 60-second timing cycle. Traffic lights for the principal road are green for 30 seconds, followed by a 5-second amber, a 20-second red, and a 5-second amber. Simple as it is, this traffic controller can be considered to be a stored-program computer.

In current interpretation, however, a stored-program computer has an additional feature: it is capable of *branching* between various segments of its program. Such branching, or *decision-making*, can be controlled by a result of previous computations; it can also be controlled by information received from an *input device* of the computer.

> **Example 1.2.** The traffic controller of Example 1.1 is expanded to include two vehicle sensors that are connected as input devices to the controller. The sensors, located on the secondary road, indicate when a vehicle is waiting for the traffic light to change. At the completion of the 30-second green light for the principal road the controller interrogates the sensors and

---

* *New terms are italicized.*

1

changes the lights only if a vehicle is waiting on the secondary road.

Stored-program digital computers have become widespread during the past two decades. This was due primarily to technological developments such as the introduction of transistors that now permeate all parts of the computer, improvements in the storage elements used in the *memory*, increased reliability of the electromechanical *peripheral devices*, and the increasing use of integrated circuits. Present-day digital computers include *special-purpose computers* tailored to a single use and *general-purpose computers* utilized in many diverse areas, such as control, data processing, and scientific calculations.

Parallel with the improved reliability, computational capability, and ease of use of general-purpose computers came the general-purpose *minicomputers* which, though limited in computational capability, were smaller and less costly. Principally because of their lower cost, minicomputers have penetrated into many applications that were previously in the exclusive domain of small special-purpose computers. The remaining gap separating general-purpose computers from special-purpose computers and controllers is being filled by the latest, and smallest, general-purpose computer, the *microcomputer*.

The first microcomputers were calculators. Now microcomputers are also replacing and augmenting many minicomputers and special-purpose computers, particularly special-purpose *hard-wired controllers*.

> **Example 1.3.** Backup safety interlocks are installed in a rapid transit system. A separate interlock is installed for each "block" of the track, monitoring the trains entering and leaving the block. In the initial demonstration each interlock used a special-purpose hard-wired controller. Because of "special cases" arising from various branches in the track, however, the controllers could not all be identical. In the final realization the hard-wired controllers are therefore replaced by microcomputers and the special cases are handled by appropriate programming.

The simplicity and reduced cost that make microcomputers widely applicable also result in programming techniques that are often difficult and clumsy compared to those required by minicomputers. Further, the circuit, or *hardware*, aspects are often more enmeshed with the programming, or *software*, aspects in a microcomputer than in a minicomputer. Thus, although the work may sometimes be divided between "hardware experts" and "software experts," the development of a system that uses a microcomputer frequently requires basic knowledge in both fields. For this reason, the two fields are interwoven in most of this book, aiming to provide a balanced introduction to hardware and software in microcomputer applications.

2

Basic Structure of Microcomputers and Microprocessors

A simplified block diagram of a microcomputer is shown in Figure 2.1. It consists of three functional blocks: the *input-output* (I/O) *section,* the *central processor unit* (CPU), and the *main memory.*[*]

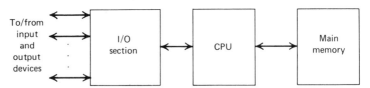

Figure 2.1. Simplified block diagram of a microcomputer.[**]

2.1. THE INPUT-OUTPUT SECTION

The lines at the left of the I/O section shown in Figure 2.1 connect the microcomputer to the *input* and *output* (I/O) *devices,* also known as *peripheral devices.*

---

[*] *A more detailed block diagram appears in Chapter 8.*
[**] Interconnecting lines in block diagrams may represent multiple connections.

Example 2.1. A handheld calculator has 10 numerical keys labeled 0 through 9, five function keys +, −, ×, ÷, and =, and six digits of decimal display, and incorporates a microcomputer that processes and stores the data. The keys are the input devices and the displayed digits are the output devices.

A simplified block diagram of an I/O section is shown in Figure 2.2. Selection of the I/O devices is performed by *input* and *output* (I/O) *multiplexers* (often abbreviated as MPX or MUX), also known as *data selectors*. Output information is stored in the *output buffers*. The *I/O register* provides temporary storage during the transmission of information between the CPU and the I/O section.

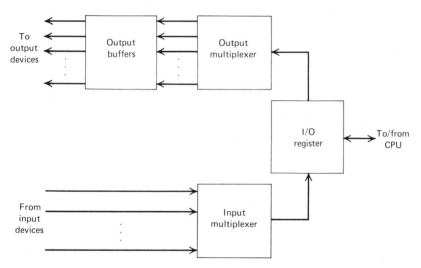

Figure 2.2. Simplified block diagram of an I/O section.

Example 2.2. A traffic controller at a street intersection uses four sensors indicating the presence of vehicles and four traffic lights. The controller incorporates a microcomputer to which the sensors are connected as input devices and the traffic lights as output devices. It is necessary to operate all four traffic lights continuously as green, amber, or red.

Since the speed of the vehicles is limited, a sensor detects a vehicle for at least 0.1 second. Thus the four sensors can be scanned sequentially by the microcomputer as long as each sensor is interrogated at a uniform rate of at least 10 readings/

second. The I/O section of the traffic controller microcomputer can be described as in Figure 2.2.

Characteristics and connections of input and output devices are discussed in Chapter 4.

2.2. THE CENTRAL PROCESSOR UNIT

The internal structure of the CPU varies widely among the various microcomputers. In what follows, we describe a simple CPU. It consists of an *arithmetic-logic unit* (ALU), several *registers,* and a *control unit* as shown in the block diagram of Figure 2.3. The number of lines interconnecting the ALU, the *accumulator* (register A), and registers B and M is determined by the *word length,* which is the maximum number of binary digits (*"bits"*) the arithmetic-logic unit can process in parallel.

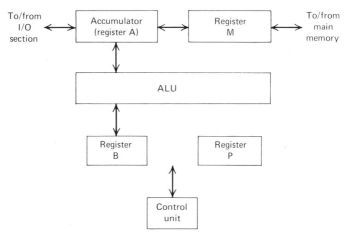

Figure 2.3. Simplified block diagram of a CPU. Connections of the control unit and register P are not shown.

The Arithmetic-Logic Unit

The ALU operates on one or two numbers. It performs arithmetic operations such as addition and subtraction, and logical operations such as the detection of equality. The structure and operation of an ALU are discussed in Chapter 6.

Registers

The CPU includes several registers often designed as *data registers, working registers,* or *scratch-pad memory.* Register A (accumulator) and register B provide storage for data operated on by the ALU.

> **Example 2.3.** In the CPU of Figure 2.3 addition is performed by adding the contents of register B to the contents of the accumulator and placing the result of the addition in the accumulator.

The bit capacity of the accumulator, as well as that of register B, are determined by the word length. In some arithmetic operations the two registers can be used together as a single register of double word length.

> **Example 2.4.** Multiplication in a CPU with a 16-bit word length is performed by multiplying the contents of the accumulator by the contents of register B. The result of the multiplication is a 32-bit number which is stored by placing the most significant 16 bits in the accumulator and the least significant 16 bits in register B.

The CPU of Figure 2.3 communicates with the I/O devices by means of the I/O section and with the main memory through register M.

> **Example 2.5.** A microcomputer incorporating the CPU of Figure 2.3 is used in an industrial temperature controller. The controller measures the temperature by means of five sensors, each of which is interrogated at a uniform rate of 12 readings/ minute. The temperature is controlled by an electric heater based on the latest 3 readings of all five temperature sensors.
> Data from the sensors are transmitted to the main memory via the I/O section, the accumulator, and register M. Temperature data from the latest 3 readings are operated on by the ALU, requiring further data transfers between the CPU and the main memory through register M. The resulting control information is sent to the heater via the I/O section.

Register P is the *program counter* determining the operating sequence of the microcomputer. The program counter counts up by one unless otherwise commanded. Each step can designate a single operation, such as the addition of two numbers, or a sequence of operations.

Example 2.6. A simple heating system consists of a thermostat, a heater that is turned on or off, and the CPU of Figure 2.3. The desired temperature is loaded into register M from the memory. The control cycle is sequenced by the program counter, that is, by register P. A simplified control sequence is outlined in Table 2.1. It is initiated once every 10 seconds by setting the contents of register P to zero.

Table 2.1. Simplified Control Sequence in the Heating System of Example 2.6

Contents of Register P	Operation
0	Start
1	Transfer the desired temperature from register M to register B
2	Read thermostat and transfer the reading into the accumulator via the I/O section
3	Compare in the ALU the contents of the accumulator with the contents of register B
4	Turn on the heater via the I/O section if the contents of the accumulator are less than the contents of register B
5	Turn off the heater via the I/O section if the contents of the accumulator are greater than or equal to the contents of register B
6	End

The Control Unit

The principal purpose of the control unit in a microcomputer is to provide suitable direction of computer operation.

Example 2.7. Addition of two numbers in the CPU of Figure 2.3 is performed as described in Example 2.3. The control unit first establishes *data paths* for sequentially routing the outputs of the accumulator and register B to the ALU and sets its operation to perform an addition. Upon completion of the addition, the control unit effects transfer of data from the ALU to the accumulator.

The operation of the control unit is discussed in Chapter 8.

2.3. THE MAIN MEMORY

The CPU and the I/O section of a microcomputer contain several registers, or *buffers*, that store changing or temporary digital information. The principal data storage in a microcomputer, however, is in its *main memory*. Compared to the registers of the CPU and the output buffers in the I/O section, the storage elements of the main memory are more numerous and usually slower.

The main memory may include several types of storage elements. The most prevalent types in microcomputers are *read-only memories* (ROMs) and *random-access memories* (RAMs). Actually both can be accessed randomly and *access times* to all locations are substantially identical. Data can be read from any location of a ROM; in a RAM, data can be read from *or* written into any location. RAM data are, however, usually destroyed upon the removal of power, while in a ROM data are preserved when the power is turned off. ROMs are therefore preferred for the storage of permanent information such as the control sequence of Table 2.1.

In general, a ROM or a RAM integrated circuit can store a large number of bits: ROM chips with storage capacities of 16,384 bits ("16-k bits") and RAM chips with storage capacities of 4096 bits ("4-k bits") are common. The storage bits in the main memory of a microcomputer are organized into *words*. Each word is identified by its *memory location*, or *address*.

> **Example 2.8.** A 2048-bit RAM and a 4096-bit ROM are used in the main memory of a microcomputer that has a word length of 8 bits. The RAM is organized into 256 words and the ROM into 512 words. Each word is identified by the address of its memory location, which may by any one of the 768 integers 0 through 767.

The elements and operation of the main memory are discussed in detail in Chapter 7.

2.4. MICROPROCESSORS

Modern technology often permits the inclusion of the entire microcomputer of Figure 2.1 on a single semiconductor chip, and some calculators have in fact been built this way. An alternate approach puts most or all of the I/O section and the CPU on a chip or on a few chips. Such chips are called *microprocessor chips, microprocessor sets,* or *microprocessors.*

To a large extent, the characteristics and limitations of a microcomputer are determined by the embedded microprocessor. Hence a thorough understanding of the properties of the microprocessor is essential to the design and use of a microcomputer.

PROBLEMS

1. How many lines are required to connect the keys and the display in the calculator of Example 2.1 assuming that no scanning of the keys or of the display is employed? Assume that each displayed digit requires 4 lines.

2. Prepare a list of the sequence of operations performing the addition of two 1-digit numbers in the calculator described in Example 2.1. Each entry in the list should represent a single operation.

3. Estimate the memory requirements for the traffic controller of Example 2.2.

4. Determine the memory requirements for the temperature controller of Example 2.5.

5. Prepare a list of operations that is equivalent to the sequence of Table 2.1 but consists only of single operations.

3

Basic Programming Techniques

The operating sequence of a microcomputer is determined by a *program,* or *code.* A program consists of a sequence of *instructions* and of *data.* Each instruction is stored in the main memory as one or more *instruction words;* data are stored as *data words.* Each instruction consists of an *operator* and some number of *operands.* The operator describes the *operation* to be performed on the data designated by the operand or operands.

> **Example 3.1.** The instruction "ADD 4" is an abbreviation for "Add to the contents of the accumulator the contents of memory location 4." The word "ADD" is the operator, and the number "4" is the operand.

The program controlling the operating sequence is stored in the main memory of the microcomputer. Each instruction is first *fetched* from the main memory and then *executed.*

> **Example 3.2.** The instruction designated by $P = 3$ in Table 2.1, "Compare in the ALU the contents of the accumulator with the contents of register B," is a *comparison instruction* that is fetched from memory location 3. It is executed by the control unit routing the outputs of the accumulator and register B to the input of the ALU and by setting it up to perform a comparison.

11

3.1. MACHINE-LANGUAGE INSTRUCTIONS

Each instruction is stored in the main memory of the microcomputer in the form of a suitable numerical code designated as a *machine-language instruction code,* which includes the operator and also the operand or operands.

> **Example 3.3.** In a microcomputer with an 8-bit word length the instruction abbreviated as "ADD 4" (see Example 3.1) is stored as a machine-language instruction code consisting of two 8-bit words. The first word is 00111000 ($= 56_{10}$), which in the given microcomputer represents the operator "ADD." The second word is 00000100 ($= 4_{10}$), which is the operand "4."*

The *instruction set* of a microcomputer may include logic, loading, storing, arithmetic, jump, and I/O instructions. Some examples of these instructions are given below; additional instructions are discussed in later chapters.

Logic Instructions

An example of logic instructions is a comparison instruction such as that in Example 3.2.

Loading Instructions

Load the contents of a specified memory location into the accumulator (*"Load accumulator"*). If the operator of this instruction is followed by the operand 00000110 ($= 6_{10}$), then the *contents* of memory location 6 are loaded into the accumulator. The contents of memory location 6 remain undisturbed.

Load a number into the accumulator (*"Load immediate"*). If the operator of this instruction is followed by the operand 00001111 ($= 15_{10}$), then the *number* 15 is loaded into the accumulator.

Storing Instructions

Store the contents of the accumulator in a specified memory location. If the operator of this instruction is followed by the operand 00001101 ($= 13_{10}$), then the contents of the accumulator are stored in memory location 13. The contents of the accumulator remain undisturbed.

---

* For explanation of notation see Section 5.1.

Arithmetic Instructions

Add to the contents of the accumulator the contents of a specified memory location. The result is stored in the accumulator; the contents of the specified memory location remain undisturbed.

Jump Instructions

Jump to a specified memory location (*"Unconditional jump"*). The contents of the program counter (register P) are changed to the specified location; hence the next instruction is fetched from that location.

Jump to a specified memory location if the content of a specified flag is a binary 1 (*"Conditional jump"*). The *flag*, which is a 1-bit register, may be an arithmetic carry, borrow, or overflow flag, or a sign or a zero flag, or some other *condition flag*.

Input-Output Instructions

Receive data from a specified input device. Data from the specified input device are loaded into the I/O register via the input multiplexer.

Send data to a specified output device. Data from the I/O register are loaded into the output buffer of the specified output device via the output multiplexer.

3.2. ASSEMBLY-LANGUAGE INSTRUCTIONS

The preceding section described machine-language instructions. A program may consist of hundreds of such instructions and must be prepared with meticulous care. A limitation arising in the use of machine-language instructions is the inability of humans to handle long binary numbers without making errors. For example, the machine-language instruction code 0011100000000100 may stand for "Add to the contents of the accumulator the contents of memory location 4" (see Examples 3.1 and 3.3). The number of mistakes in copying such an instruction code can be reduced considerably by use of a *mnemonic* abbreviation such as "ADD 4," as was done in Examples 3.1 and 3.3. A programming language in which each machine-language instruction code is replaced by a mnemonic abbreviation is designated an *assembly language* or *symbolic language*.

To obtain a program in machine-language as required by the microcomputer, a program that was written in an assembly language must

be translated; this translation is performed by an *assembler* program.*
The assembler can be *resident* in the main memory of the microcomputer or it can be a *cross-assembler* that is located in a different—probably larger—computer.

> **Example 3.4.** A program for a microcomputer is written in an assembly language by using a paper-tape punch controlled by a typewriterlike keyboard. The resulting roll of tape is read into a large computer by use of a paper-tape reader as an input device. A cross-assembler program that is written in a language suitable for the large computer is also read in. The large computer translates the assembly-language program into a machine-language program for the microcomputer as directed by the cross-assembler program. The resulting machine-language program is punched out by the large computer on paper tape, which is then read into the microcomputer.

Macroinstructions

Once an assembler is available that translates assembly-language instructions into machine-language instructions, we can use it for other tasks. For example, a large group of instructions that is repeated many times in the program can be defined as a *macroinstruction,* and then be used instead of the group. The assembler substitutes the group of instructions for the macroinstruction as required.

> **Example 3.5.** A group of 20 instructions occurs 10 times in an assembly-language program. To save writing, we define a macroinstruction named MAC1 as follows:
>
> DEFINE MACRO MACI
>
> $\left.\begin{array}{l} \cdots \\ \cdots \\ \cdots \end{array}\right\}$ (list of the 20 instructions defining MAC1)
>
> END
>
> Subsequently we write MAC1 in 10 different places in the program. The assembler substitutes the 20 instructions for each of the 10 MAC1's as it encounters them.

---

* *More details on assemblers are given in Chapter 9.*

Thus the use of macroinstructions does not alter the resulting machine-language program, but saves repeated writing of a long sequence of instructions in the assembly-language program. An unfortunate side effect in using macroinstructions is that the assembly-language program may look deceptively short. Hence care must be exercised in estimating the program size (memory space allocation) whenever macroinstructions are used.

> **Example 3.6.** An assembly-language program consists of 30 instructions, of which 12 are MAC1 macroinstructions defined in Example 3.5 (without the DEFINE and END instructions). The machine-language program assembled by the assembler thus consists of 258 machine-language instructions, exceeding the 256 memory locations that are available in the particular micro-computer.

3.3. HIGHER-LEVEL PROGRAMMING LANGUAGES

The use of an assembly language represents an improvement over a machine language for the programmer who must write or understand a program. Nevertheless, a significant amount of writing still remains, and even simple programs, such as that illustrated in Example 2.6, may require tens of instructions.

The work of the programmer has been further alleviated by the introduction of *higher-level programming languages*. These programming languages combine several instructions into a *statement*, and a sequence of statements constitutes a program.

> **Example 3.7.** In ALGOL, a higher-level programming language, the statement $Y \leftarrow Z$ means: "The value of Z is assigned to Y." A more complex statement is the following: IF $V > W$ THEN $X \leftarrow Y - 1$ ELSE $X \leftarrow Y + 1$.

A program written in a higher-level programming language is usually much shorter than one written in an assembly language, and may be even shorter than the original presentation of the problem.

> **Example 3.8.** The program of Example 2.6 can be written in ALGOL as follows:

BEGIN
$A \leftarrow THERMOSTAT;$

$B \leftarrow M$;
IF $A < B$ THEN *HEATER* $\leftarrow 1$ ELSE *HEATER* $\leftarrow 0$;
END.

A higher-level programming language is translated into a machine language by a *compiler* program. The compiler inspects each statement, assigns memory locations for the storage of variables and constants, and generates the machine-language instructions.

An important question that arises in connection with the operation of a compiler is its efficiency. Since it is only a program that operates in a routine manner, the machine-language program it generates usually consists of considerably more instructions and may use more memory locations than does the machine-language program written by a skilled programmer. This inefficiency may be more critical in a small microcomputer, although it may also be significant in larger computers. For this reason the programmer is often given the option of combining assembly language and higher-level programming language in a single program.

3.4. SUBROUTINES

We have already seen that the use of macroinstructions simplifies the writing of an assembly-language program but that the resulting machine-language program is not altered. When a sequence of instructions or statements occurs many times in a program, it may preferably be part of the machine-language program only once and should be referred to, or *called*, whenever it is needed. Such a sequence of instructions is designated a *subroutine*, also known as *procedure*. It can be written in a machine language, an assembly language, or a higher-level programming language. When used many times in a program, a subroutine provides significant savings in memory space.

> **Example 3.9.** The solution for a root of a quadratic equation, $ROOT = (-B + \sqrt{B^2 - 4AC})/2A$, is used 100 times in a program, each time with different values of A, B, and C. A subroutine computing $ROOT$ may be written in ALGOL as follows:

```
PROCEDURE ROOT (A, B, C);
ROOT ← 0;
D ← B × B − 4 × A × C;
IF D ≧ 0 THEN ROOT ← (−B + SQRT(D))/(2 × A);
PRINT (A, B, C, D, ROOT);
END;
```

Note that SQRT(D) stands for $\sqrt{D}$ computed by a separate subroutine when $D \geq 0$. When $D < 0$, the printout will show a *ROOT* = 0 and the negative value of D, thus indicating that the correct (complex) *ROOT* cannot be computed by this simple procedure.

The savings in memory space attained by the use of a subroutine are somewhat reduced by the overhead incurred in the memory space and the execution time of the *subroutine linkage* required for the call of the subroutine and for the *return* from it. Subroutine linkages are discussed in Chapter 9.

3.5. FLOW CHARTS

An important tool in the development of a program is the *flow chart*. Unless the programmer is very experienced and the problem at hand is very simple, it is desirable to first draw a flow chart based on the original presentation of the problem and then proceed to write the program. Selected *elements* of flow charts are shown in Figure 3.1. A flow chart may consist of any combination of these elements.

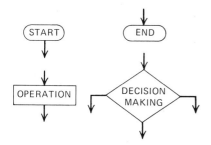

Figure 3.1. Selected elements of flow charts.

Example 3.10. A subroutine for finding a root of a quadratic equation was described in Example 3.9. A flow chart for the subroutine is shown in Figure 3.2. It consists of seven blocks: one START, one END, four OPERATION, and one DECISION MAKING.

Each element in a flow chart may be passed through any finite number of times during the execution of the program except that a START or an END may be passed through only once. An important structure for the

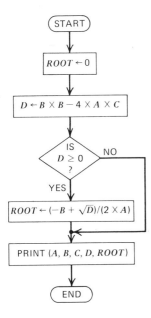

Figure 3.2. Flow chart for finding a root of a quadratic equation.

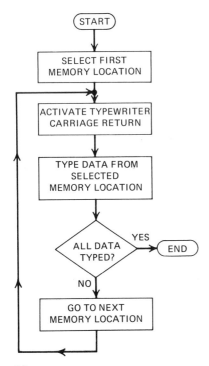

Figure 3.3. Flow chart of a program for typing the contents of a block of memory locations.

18

multiple execution of a program segment is the *loop,* also known as *DO loop.*

> **Example 3.11.** Figure 3.3 shows a flow chart of a program that types out the contents of a block of memory locations. After selecting the first memory location to be typed, it types the contents of each location by passing through the loop in the flow chart until all data are typed out.

PROBLEMS

1. The machine-language instruction code for the operator of the "load accumulator" instruction is 00001000, and for the "load immediate" it is 00001001. The contents of memory location 11_{10} is 5_{10}. What are the contents of the accumulator after the execution of each of the following instructions: 0000100000001011, 0000100100001011, and 0000100111111111?

2. Specify a set of mnemonic abbreviations and write an assembly-language program for the heating system of Example 2.6.

3. Summarize the advantages and possible disadvantages of programs written in a machine language, an assembly language, and a higher-level programming language.

4. Discuss the advantages and possible disadvantages of a subroutine as compared with a macroinstruction.

5. Draw a flow chart and outline a subroutine for computing the average of the four numbers A, B, C, and D.

6. Prepare a flow chart for the operation of the temperature controller described in Example 2.5.

7. How many memory locations are required in the program of Example 3.6 if the macroinstructions are replaced by a subroutine? Include one call instruction for each subroutine call and one return instruction in the subroutine.

4

Input and Output

Communication between the computer and the outside world is through *I/O devices,* also known as *peripheral devices.* This chapter discusses the structure of instructions used for the operation of I/O devices, the structure and operation of the I/O section, interconnection of I/O devices, interrupts, and direct memory access.*

4.1. INPUT AND OUTPUT INSTRUCTIONS

The I/O instructions of a microcomputer were described in Section 3.1 as "Data from the specified input device are loaded into the I/O register via the input multiplexer" and "Data from the I/O register are loaded into the output buffer of the specified output device via the output multiplexer." These instructions handle the transfer of data as well as *control information.* Control *information* may include a "ready" signal from the printer mechanism of an electric typewriter, an "end of card" signal from a punched-card reader, a "ready for next card" signal from a card punch, a "rewind" command to a magnetic-tape unit, a "rewind completed," or an "end of tape" signal from a magnetic-tape unit, and others. Various microcomputers permit, or require, a varying degree of programmer involvement in handling the control information that must be included in the I/O instructions.

---

* *A detailed description of peripheral devices can be found in reference 2.*

4.2. THE INPUT-OUTPUT SECTION

The basic components of the I/O section, which is also known as *I/O controller,* were given in Figure 2.2 as the I/O register, the I/O multiplexers, and the output buffers. This section presents more details on the operation of these circuits.

The Input-Output Register

The I/O register handles the transmission of information between the I/O section and the CPU of the microcomputer. When the bit capacity of the I/O register is inadequate for the simultaneous transmission of data, control information, and *device identification,* transmission takes place in sequential groups.

> **Example 4.1.** A microcomputer with an 8-bit word length has 16 I/O devices, some requiring 4 bits of control information. Thus the I/O section, hence the I/O register, has to handle 4 bits of coded device identification and 4 bits of control information in addition to the 8 bits of data. These are handled in two subsequent groups: the first group of 8 bits consists of the 4 bits of device identification and the 4 bits of control information, and the second group consists of 8 bits of data.

A significant feature of the I/O register is that it provides for *bidirectional* data flow; this is illustrated for a single bit in the circuit of Figure 4.1. The storage element in the circuit is a D flip-flop whose next state is set by clock C to the present state of input D. Also used are logic circuits with *3-state outputs* that present an open circuit when the *ENABLE* input (frequently also designated as $\overline{INHIBIT}$) is logical 0.* The *DIRECTION* input determines whether data flow is to the right or to the left, provided that the *ACTIVATE* input permits data flow.

Multiplexers and Buffers

As mentioned in Section 2.1, a microcomputer may include several *multiplexers.* The structure of a multiplexer is governed by whether its data flow is only in one direction or in both directions. In the simple case of the I/O section of Figure 2.2, the input and output multiplexers are both *undirectional,* but their structures are different.

* *More details on digital circuits can be found in reference 1.*

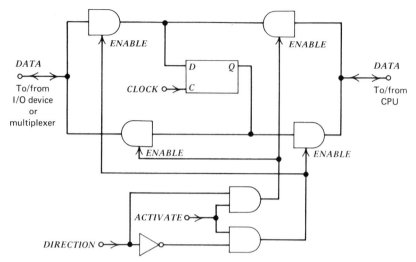

Figure 4.1. Bidirectional data flow of 1 bit in an I/O register.

The circuit diagram of a unidirectional input multiplexer is shown in Figure 4.2. It handles three input devices with 4-bit word lengths. Merging of data is accomplished by logic circuits with 3-state outputs that are activated by one of three *ENABLE* inputs; only one *ENABLE* input is allowed to be a binary 1 at any given time.

A circuit diagram of a unidirectional output multiplexer, which includes output buffers, is shown in Figure 4.3. It consists of *D-E flip-flops* whose next state is set by clock *C* to the present state of input *D* if *ENABLE* input *E* is at logical 1; the state remains unchanged irrespective of *D* if *E* is at logical 0. The *ENABLE* (*E*) inputs belonging to the same input device are connected in parallel.

> **Example 4.2.** In the I/O section of the traffic controller of Example 2.2 the input devices are separated from the output devices. Thus multiplexers similar to those of Figures 4.2 and 4.3 can be used.

When the lines connecting the input and output devices are not separated, a *bidirectional* multiplexer must be utilized. The basic circuit of a bidirectional multiplexer is identical to Figure 4.1, and its use is illustrated in Figure 4.4. All *DIRECTION* (*DIR*) inputs for a given device are connected in parallel, as well as all *ACTIVATE* (*A*) inputs. A device

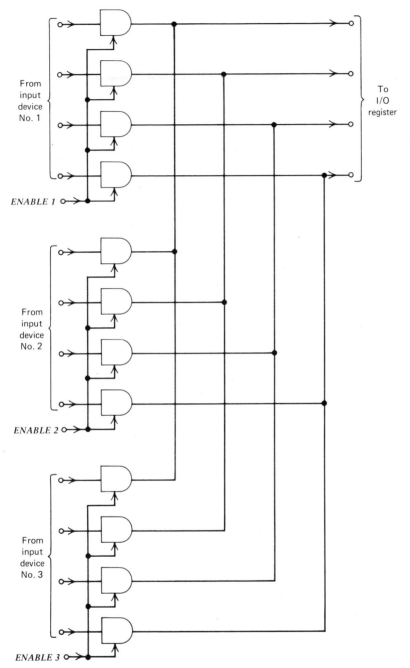

Figure 4.2. Unidirectional input multiplexer using logic circuits with 3-state outputs.

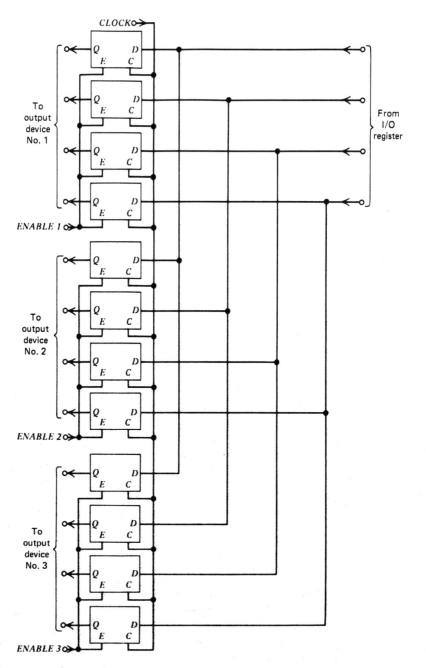

Figure 4.3. Unidirectional output multiplexer and output buffers using D-E flip-flops.

24

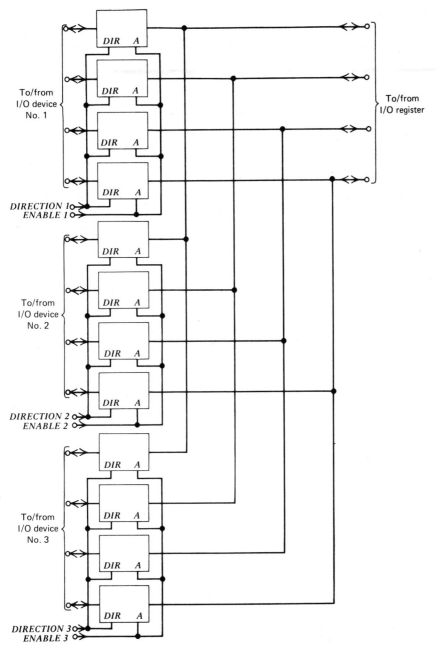

Figure 4.4. Bidirectional I/O multiplexing. Each of the 12 blocks represents the circuit of Figure 4.1 with *DIRECTION* marked as *DIR*, *ACTIVATE* as *A*, and the *DATA* lines unmarked.

25

is selected by making its *ENABLE* a binary 1; only one of the *ENABLE* lines is allowed to be a binary 1 at any given time.

Control information can be handled together with data when both flow in the same direction. Otherwise data and control information of a device can be treated as if they belonged to two separate devices with opposite directions of data flow. The situation is similar when the flow of control information is bidirectional (*"handshake"* operation).

The overall structure of an I/O section is outlined in Figure 4.5. It includes an *auxiliary multiplexer* that transfers the I/O device indentification to the *I/O device ID register* and also provides bidirectional transfer of data and control information between the *I/O data register* and the I/O register. The auxiliary multiplexer is not required in microcomputers that have separate data and address *bus lines*. The contents of the I/O

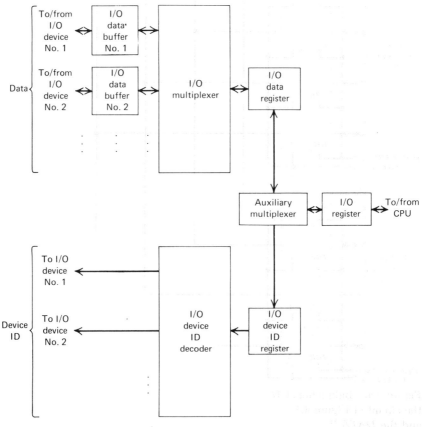

Figure 4.5. Simplified overall diagram of an I/O section.

device ID register are decoded by the *I/O device ID decoder*. In some installations, especially when many I/O devices are involved, it may be more economical to locate these decoders, as well as the *I/O data buffers*, at the I/O devices rather than in the microcomputer. The decision must be based on several factors, such as the number of I/O devices, the word length, the location of the I/O devices with respect to the microcomputer, and the available integrated circuits.

4.3. INTERRUPTS

So far computing and I/O operations have been interleaved by operating the I/O devices under program control (*polling*). In another mode of operation, an I/O device may request servicing by sending an *interrupt request* signal to the microcomputer.

> **Example 4.3.** The operation of the temperature controller of Example 2.5 is directed through an electric typewriter by typing the desired temperature and activating the carriage return. Every time a digit, a decimal point, a letter, or a carriage return is entered through the keyboard, the typewriter requests processing of the information it received by sending an interrupt request signal to the microcomputer.

Upon receipt of an interrupt request signal, the microcomputer completes the instruction in progress and calls an *interrupt subroutine*. In some microcomputers, one of several interrupt subroutines may be selected by dedicated circuitry (*vectored interrupt*). Control is returned from the interrupt subroutine to the normal instruction sequence after the servicing of the input device has been completed.

Interrupt requests may also be issued by output devices. Some output devices, such as a paper-tape punch, can wait indefinitely for the microprocessor to supply the next character and thus can utilize either polling or interrupt. However, other output devices, such as a magnetic-tape unit, may require servicing within a certain time, hence must use interrupt for prompt attention.

> **Example 4.4.** A low-cost cassette tape recorder is started by a start command from the microcomputer. After attaining its normal operating speed, it records 1000 characters/second.
> Every time it is ready to record a character, the cassette recorder sends an interrupt request signal to the microcomputer

requesting the next character. For correct operation of the tape unit, the microcomputer must service this interrupt within a time period of about 1 millisecond.

Many microcomputers provide a *multiple interrupt* system, to which several I/O devices may be connected. The devices may be assigned equal or different *priorities* in obtaining access by interrupt.

4.4. DIRECT MEMORY ACCESS

Direct memory access (DMA) bypasses the I/O section and provides high-speed direct data transfers in either direction between the main memory and a peripheral device. Operation of the I/O section and of the CPU usually halt during DMA, and memory control is performed by an external DMA logic circuit. The necessity for this external circuitry, however, offsets somewhat the advantage gained in increased speed; as a result, DMA is installed primarily when high-speed transfer of large blocks of data is required.

PROBLEMS

1. Determine the direction of data flow in Figure 4.1 when the *DIRECTION* input is a binary 1.
2. Sketch a timing diagram for the signals in the bidirectional multiplexer of Figure 4.4 operating one input and two output devices sequentially.
3. Extend the timing diagram of Problem 2 to include the *DIRECTION* and *ACTIVATE* signals of the I/O register.
4. Sketch a logic circuit showing the details of the I/O section of Figure 4.5. Assume 3 peripheral devices and a word length of 4 bits.
5. Sketch a timing diagram for the signals in the circuit of Problem 4 operating one input and two output devices sequentially.
6. The I/O data buffers and the I/O device ID decoder may be located in the microcomputer or at the I/O devices. Consider the factors involved in this tradeoff.
7. Outline a reasonable priority sequence among an electric typewriter, a cassette tape recorder, and a paper-tape punch. Sketch a circuit that handles the multiple interrupts and that also provides the microcomputer with the identification of the I/O device requesting the interrupt.

Arithmetic Operations

This chapter describes the various *number systems* utilized in micro-computers, as well as *floating-point representation* and *floating-point arithmetic*. It also discusses several *coding techniques,* including the *ASCII code,* for representing the *characters* of the alphabet and other symbols.

5.1. NUMBER SYSTEMS

The number system in everyday use employs the *decimal base* and a *positional notation;* that is, every digit in a multidigit word has a *weight* attached to it. For example, the decimal number 4956 may be expressed as the sum of weighted coefficients: $4956 = 4 \times 10^3 + 9 \times 10^2 + 5 \times 10^1 + 6 \times 10^0$.

The decimal base is not the only base in which numbers can be ex-pressed. Thus, because of the binary nature of computer circuits, the *binary number system* has found wide acceptance. This system uses only 0's and 1's, thus $1 + 0 = 0 + 1 = 1$; $1 + 1 = 10$ (read: zero carry one); $10 + 1 = 11$, and so on. The rules of arithmetic operations are similar to those of the decimal system, except that the binary number system uses a set of of two binary digits $\{0, 1\}$ instead of the set of ten decimal digits $\{0, 1, \ldots, 9\}$.

In general, any number N_b that consists of n digits and is given in any base b can be expressed as the sum of its weighted coefficients:

$$N_b = a_{n-1}b^{n-1} + a_{n-2}b^{n-2} + \cdots + a_1b^1 + a_0b^0 = \sum_{i=0}^{n-1} a_ib^i. \quad (5.1)$$

.ional notation the weights are only implied. Thus

$$N_b = a_{n-1}a_{n-2} \cdots a_1a_0. \tag{5.2}$$

Binary Numbers

Binary numbers use the base 2 and are often denoted by a subscript 2. For example, 11_2 expresses a number in binary notation that is equivalent to the decimal 3_{10}. Because of the extensive use of both the binary and the decimal number systems, *number base conversions* between these bases will be described in detail. A number given in one base can be expressed by an equivalent numerical value in another base by the application of a *conversion algorithm*.

Binary-to-Decimal Conversion

Two methods for binary-to-decimal conversion are presented here. One of these is based on eq. 5.1 and is illustrated by Examples 5.1 and 5.2.

Example 5.1. Convert to base 10 the binary integer number $N_2 = 111001_2$.
  Based on eq. 5.1, N_2 represents the sum
$N_2 = 1 \times 2^5 + 1 \times 2^4 + 1 \times 2^3 + 0 \times 2^2 + 0 \times 2^1 + 1 \times 2^0.$
Hence
$N_2 = (32 + 16 + 8 + 1)_{10} = 57_{10}.$

Fractional numbers may be converted in a similar manner by remembering that the value of each binary digit, or *bit*, after the *binary point* changes by a factor of $\frac{1}{2}$. Equation 5.1 can thus be extended to include fractional bits that are placed to the right of the binary point. Assigning to these coefficients the subscripts $a_{-1}, a_{-2}, \ldots, a_{-m}$, results in

$$N_2 \text{ (fractional)} = a_{-1}2^{-1} + a_{-2}2^{-2} + \cdots + a_{-m+1} 2^{-m+1} + a_{-m} 2^{-m}$$

$$= \sum_{i=-m}^{-1} a_i 2^i. \tag{5.3}$$

Example 5.2. Convert to base 10 the binary fraction $N_2 = 0.11001_2$:

$N_2 \text{ (fractional)} = 1 \times 2^{-1} + 1 \times 2^{-2} + 0 \times 2^{-3} + 0 \times 2^{-4} + 1 \times 2^{-5} = (0.5 + 0.25 + 0.03125)_{10} = 0.78125_{10}.$

Another way to convert a binary number to a decimal number which is applicable only to integer numbers is the "*double-dabble*" method. It is based on the following nested representation of binary numbers:

$$N_2 = \{[(a_{n-1} \cdot 2 + a_{n-2}) \cdot 2 + a_{n-3}] \cdot 2 + \cdots + a_1\} \cdot 2 + a_0. \quad (5.4)$$

Equation 5.4 shows the conversion procedure. The *most significant bit* (msb) is doubled and then added to the coefficient of the next bit, which may be 0 or 1. The result is doubled again, and the procedure is terminated when the *least significant* bit (lsb) has been finally added.

> **Example 5.3.** To convert the binary number 1001101 to its decimal equivalent by use of the double-dabble method we proceed as illustrated in Figure 5.1.

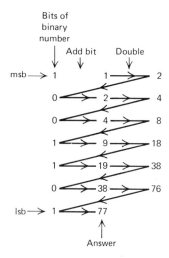

Figure 5.1. Binary-to-decimal conversion using the double-dabble method.

Decimal-to-Binary Conversion

One method for decimal-to-binary conversion by hand that is convenient for small numbers, integer or fractional, is based on recognition of the powers of 2 contained in the decimal number. It starts by subtracting the highest power of 2 contained in the decimal number to be converted and continues until the conversion has been completed.

> **Example 5.4.** To convert 167_{10} to a binary number we note that 2^7 is the highest power of 2 contained in the number to be

converted. Thus $167 - 2^7 = 167 - 128 = 39$. Also now $39 - 2^5 = 7 = 111_2$. Hence the answer is $167 = 2^7 + 2^5 + 2^2 + 2^1 + 2^0$; that is, $167_{10} = 10100111_2$.

This method is cumbersome for large numbers. Another decimal-to-binary conversion procedure calls for successive division by 2 of the decimal integer number; the remainders represent the binary number, the first remainder being the least significant bit.

Example 5.5. To convert the integer number 167_{10} to a binary representation we proceed as follows:

	Remainder	Binary Weight
$167 \div 2 = 83$	1	2^0 (lsb)
$83 \div 2 = 41$	1	2^1
$41 \div 2 = 20$	1	2^2
$20 \div 2 = 10$	0	2^3
$10 \div 2 = 5$	0	2^4
$5 \div 2 = 2$	1	2^5
$2 \div 2 = 1$	0	2^6
$1 \div 2 = 0$	1	2^7 (msb)

The answer is obtained by reading the remainder column from bottom to top: $167_{10} = 10100111_2$.

When the number is fractional it is successively multiplied by 2 and the result is obtained by reading the *carry* column from top to bottom. Not every rational decimal fraction can be converted to a binary fraction of finite number of bits and a *round-off* error results when the process is terminated.

Example 5.6. To convert 0.57_{10} to a binary fraction we proceed as follows:

	Carry	Binary Weight
$0.57 \times 2 = 1.14$	1	2^{-1} (msb)
$0.14 \times 2 = 0.28$	0	2^{-2}
$0.28 \times 2 = 0.56$	0	2^{-3}
$0.56 \times 2 = 1.12$	1	2^{-4}
$0.12 \times 2 = 0.24$	0	2^{-5}
$0.24 \times 2 = 0.48$	0	2^{-6}
$0.48 \times 2 = 0.96$	0	2^{-7}
$0.96 \times 2 = 1.92$	1	2^{-8}

At this point we arbitrarily cut off the process. The result, by reading the carry column from top to bottom, is $0.57_{10} = 0.10010001 + \epsilon$, with a round-off error of $\epsilon < 2^{-8} = 1/256$.

Conversion of a mixed number consisting of integer and fractional parts can be performed as follows. First the integer and fractional parts are separated, next the conversion of the integer and fractional parts is effected by the respective conversion algorithms, and finally the two results are appropriately merged.

Negative Number Representations

Thus far we have considered binary integer and fractional numbers without regard to their sign. In what follows we describe three representations in which positive and negative numbers can be distinguished. Each of these three representations uses an additional *sign bit*, which becomes the leftmost bit of the *signed binary number*. The three representations are the *sign-and-magnitude representation, the 1's-complement representation,* and the *2's-complement representation.*

Sign-and-Magnitude Representation. The magnitude of the number in this representation is expressed in the binary form of eq. 5.1. The sign bit placed to the left of the most significant bit represents a "+" when 0 and a "−" when 1. Thus the positive number $+5.25_{10}$ is represented by 0 101.01 and the negative number -5.25_{10} by 1 101.01. A binary number of n integer and m fractional bits expressed in sign-and-magnitude representation by $n + m + 1$ bits has a value of

$$N = (-1)^{b_n} \cdot \left(\sum_{i=0}^{n-1} b_i 2^i + \sum_{i=-m}^{-1} b_i 2^i \right)$$

$$= (-1)^{b_n} \cdot \sum_{i=-m}^{n-1} b_i 2^i, \tag{5.5}$$

where b_i are the binary coefficients 0 or 1.

This representation, although easily readable, does not lend itself to easy implementation in digital arithmetic circuits for several reasons. For one, there are two different expressions of the number zero: $000\cdots0$ and $100\cdots0$. Also, when adding a positive and a negative number we must first check the magnitudes of both numbers, subtract the smaller magnitude from the larger one, and then assign to the result the sign of the number that had the larger magnitude.

1's-Complement Representation. In the 1's-complement representation positive numbers are expressed in the same way as in the sign-and-magnitude representation. The convention of the sign bit is also the same in both representations, namely 0 for "+" and 1 for "−." However, to express the magnitude part of a negative number in the 1's-complement representation, we have to take its *1's complement* (also known as *complement*). The 1's complement of a number is obtained by *logical inversion* of each bit in the number, that is, by changing all 0's to 1's and all 1's to 0's. Note that the complement of a complemented number is the number itself. Also note that the sign bit, which is the most significant bit, is (unlike in the sign-and-magnitude representation) treated in addition and subtraction the same way as the bits representing the magnitude.

> **Example 5.7.** The positive number $+5.25_{10}$ is expressed in 1's-complement representation as $0\ 101.01_2$—the same as in sign-and-magnitude representation. To express -5.25_{10} in 1's-complement representation, we first complement the magnitude—we take the complement of 101.01_2 which is 010.10—and then assign a minus sign bit (which is 1) to the left of the most significant bit. Thus in 1's-complement representation $-5.25_{10} = 1\ 010.10_2$.

It can be shown that a binary number of n integer and m fractional bits expressed in 1's-complement representation by $n + m + 1$ bits has a value of

$$N = (1 - b_n) \cdot \sum_{i=-m}^{n-1} b_i 2^i - b_n \cdot \sum_{i=-m}^{n-1} (1 - b_i)\, 2^i, \qquad (5.6)$$

where b_i are the binary coefficients 0 or 1. Note that $1 - b_i$ is the 1's complement of the ith bit. Also, for positive numbers the second term on the right side of eq. 5.6 reduces to zero and, conversely, for negative numbers the first term becomes zero.

Also note that (as was the case in sign-and-magnitude representation) in the 1's-complement representation there are two different expressions for the number 0, which are now, however, $00 \ldots 0$ and $11 \ldots 1$.

2's-Complement Representation. The 2's-complement representation of numbers is widely used in microcomputers. Positive numbers are expressed identically in the sign-and-magnitude, in the 1's-complement, and in the 2's-complement representations. Also, the sign bit is the same in the three representations: 0 for "+" and 1 for "−." To express the magnitude part of a number in the 2's-complement representation, we have to take its *2's complement*. The 2's complement of a number may be obtained by first deriving its 1's complement and then adding 1 to the least significant bit, be it integer or fractional. Note that (as was the case in the 1's-complement representation) in addition and subtraction the sign bit is treated the same way as the bits representing the magnitude.

Example 5.8. (a) The 2's complement of $58_{10} = 111010_2$ is derived as follows:

$$58_{10} = 0 \ 111010$$
$$\text{1's complement of } 58_{10} = 1 \ 000101$$
$$\text{add 1 to lsb : } 1 \quad \Big\} \ \text{add}$$

result: 2's complement of $58_{10} = 1 \ 000110$

(b) The 2's complement of 42.5_{10} is derived as follows:

$$42.5_{10} = 0 \ 101010.1$$
$$\text{1's complement of } 42.5_{10} = 1 \ 010101.0$$
$$\text{add 1 to lsb : } 1 \quad \Big\} \ \text{add}$$

result: 2's complement of $42.5_{10} = 1 \ 010101.1$

It can be shown that a binary number consisting of n integer and m fractional bits expressed in 2's-complement representation by $n + m + 1$ bits has a value of

$$N = (1 - b_n) \cdot \sum_{i=-m}^{n-1} b_i 2^i - b_n \cdot \sum_{i=-m}^{n-1} [(1 - b_i)2^i] + 2^{-m}. \quad (5.7)$$

For integer numbers eq. 5.7 reduces to

$$N = (1 - b_n) \cdot \sum_{i=0}^{n-1} b_i 2^i - b_n \cdot \sum_{i=0}^{n-1} [(1 - b_i)2^i] + 1. \quad (5.8)$$

Note that, unlike the other two representations, the 2's-complement representation has only one expression for the number 0, namely

0 00 ··· 0. Table 5.1 shows several numbers expressed in the three representations discussed above.

5.2. OCTAL AND HEXADECIMAL NUMBER REPRESENTATIONS

A long string of 1's and 0's that represents a certain numerical value is
not easily handled by a human operator. There are two generally
adopted solutions to this problem: *coding* (or *encoding*), which is discussed in the next section, and the use of numbers whose base is some
integer power of 2, such as *octal numbers* (base 2^3) and *hexadecimal
numbers* (base 2^4).

The Octal Number System

In this system the base $b = 2^3 = 8_{10}$; thus eight *symbols* 0 through 7 are
required to express any number. An octal number N_8 consisting of n
integer and m fractional digits can be represented by the sum

$$N_8 = a_{n-1}8^{n-1} + a_{n-2}8^{n-2} + \cdots + a_1 8^1 + a_0 8^0 + a_{-1}8^{-1} + \cdots$$

$$+ a_{-m}8^{-m} = \sum_{i=-m}^{n-1} a_i 8^i. \tag{5.9}$$

The eight combinations for the eight symbols used in the octal number
system can be represented by exactly 3 binary bits. Thus conversion of a
binary number to an octal number can be performed by the following
rule: arrange the integer part of the binary number in groups of 3,
starting with the rightmost integer bit; the fractional part is grouped
similarly but starting with the leftmost fractional bit.

Example 5.9. To convert the binary number 11100011.1011 to
an octal number we have

leading 0 is implied

trailing 0's are implied

Binary: 011 100 011 . 101 100
Octal: 3   4   3 . 5   4

Octal representations of selected number are given in Table 5.2.

Table 5.1 Three Binary Representations of Selected Numbers

Decimal Number	Sign-and-Magnitude Representation	1's-Complement Representation	2's-Complement Representation
+7	0 111	0 111	0 111
+6	0 110	0 110	0 110
+5	0 101	0 101	0 101
+4	0 100	0 100	0 100
+3	0 011	0 011	0 011
+2	0 010	0 010	0 010
+1	0 001	0 001	0 001
0	$\begin{cases} 0\ 000 \\ 1\ 000 \end{cases}$	$\begin{cases} 0\ 000 \\ 1\ 111 \end{cases}$	0 000
−1	1 001	1 110	1 111
−2	1 010	1 101	1 110
−3	1 011	1 100	1 101
−4	1 100	1 011	1 100
−5	1 101	1 010	1 011
−6	1 110	1 001	1 010
−7	1 111	1 000	1 001

Table 5.2 Decimal, Binary, Octal, and Hexadecimal Number Representations

Decimal	Binary	Octal	Hexadecimal
0	0000	0	0
1	0001	1	1
2	0010	2	2
3	0011	3	3
4	0100	4	4
5	0101	5	5
6	0110	6	6
7	0111	7	7
8	1000	10	8
9	1001	11	9
10	1010	12	A
11	1011	13	B
12	1100	14	C
13	1101	15	D
14	1110	16	E
15	1111	17	F
16	10000	20	10

The Hexadecimal Number System

In this system the base $b = 2^4$; thus 4 bits are required to express one hexadecimal digit and there are $2^4 = 16_{10}$ symbols. These symbols are 0, 1, 2, 3, 4, 5, 6, 7, 8, 9, A, B, C, D, E, F; A represents ten, B eleven, and so on until F, that represents fifteen. Hexadecimal representations of selected numbers are shown in Table 5.2.

The 16 different combinations (symbols) can be represented by exactly 4 bits. Thus a rule for converting a binary number to a hexadecimal number is as follows: arrange the integer part of the binary number in groups of 4, starting with the rightmost integer bit; the fractional part is similarly grouped, but starting with the leftmost fractional bit.

> **Example 5.10.** To convert the binary number 11100011.1011
> ($= 227.6875_{10}$) to a hexadecimal number we have:
> Binary: 1110   0011 . 1011
> Hexadecimal: E   3   .   B

Comparison of Number Systems

A number N may be expressed in binary representation by b digits, in octal representation by e digits, in decimal representation by d digits, and in hexadecimal representation by h digits, where N, b, e, d, and h are related as

$$N = 2^b{}_{10} = 8^e{}_{10} = 10^d{}_{10} = 16^h{}_{10}. \tag{5.10}$$

From eq. 5.10 it also follows that

$$\frac{e}{b} = 3, \quad \frac{h}{b} = 4, \quad \frac{h}{e} = \frac{4}{3}, \quad \frac{b}{d} = \frac{1}{\log_{10}2} = 3.32, \quad \frac{e}{d} = \frac{1}{\log_{10}8} = 1.05,$$

$$\frac{h}{d} = \frac{1}{\log_{10}16} = 0.895. \tag{5.11}$$

The binary-to-decimal conversion described in Example 5.5 repeatedly divided the integer decimal number by 2 to obtain the equivalent binary number. A generalization of this procedure is the following. If a number in base b_1 is to be converted to a number in base b_2, the conversion arithmetic must be carried out in base b_1. Furthermore, conversion of integer numbers requires repeated division while the conversion of fractional numbers requires repeated multiplication. Thus conversion from octal or from hexadecimal to decimal utilizes addition and multiplication in octal or hexadecimal, respectively.

Such conversions and octal and hexadecimal arithmetic operations are facilitated by use of the addition and multiplication tables given in Appendices A and B.

5.3. CODING

There are four principal applications for coding in a microcomputer: (1) reduction of the number of digits to a level that can be conveniently handled by a human operator; (2) coding the 1's and 0's to obtain binary-coded decimal numbers that are convenient as I/O representations; (3) coding to detect errors originating during transmission of information between various parts of a computer system; and (4) coding to represent in binary form characters of the alphabet and other symbols, including those required for communication between the computer and its peripheral devices (for example, "carriage return" of an electric typewriter).

Coding to Reduce the Number of Digits

The octal and hexadecimal numbers discussed in Section 5.2 are good examples of number representations that require fewer digits than does the binary number representation.

> **Example 5.11.** The number of digits required to express an integer number in octal representation is a factor of 3 less than in the binary representation, while the hexadecimal representation results in a reduction by a factor of 4.

Binary-Coded Decimal Numbers

The binary-coded decimal (BCD) representation utilizes 4 binary bits to express 10 combinations for the decimal numbers 0 through 9. Actually, 4 binary bits could represent as many as 16 numbers (states). Thus a redundancy exists that permits many different BCD codes. Three such codes are shown in Table 5.3. The most commonly used BCD code is

Table 5.3   BCD Numbers

Decimal Number	BCD 8421	BCD 2421	BCD Excess-3
0	0 0 0 0	0 0 0 0	0 0 1 1
1	0 0 0 1	0 0 0 1	0 1 0 0
2	0 0 1 0	0 0 1 0	0 1 0 1
3	0 0 1 1	0 0 1 1	0 1 1 0
4	0 1 0 0	0 1 0 0	0 1 1 1
5	0 1 0 1	1 0 1 1	1 0 0 0
6	0 1 1 0	1 1 0 0	1 0 0 1
7	0 1 1 1	1 1 0 1	1 0 1 0
8	1 0 0 0	1 1 1 0	1 0 1 1
9	1 0 0 1	1 1 1 1	1 1 0 0

the 8-4-2-1 or *naturally-weighted binary-coded decimal* shown in column 2 of the table. Column 3 shows the *2-4-2-1 BCD code*, while the last column shows the *excess-3 BCD code*, which is derived from the 8-4-2-1 BCD code by adding 3_{10} to each coded number. The latter two codes have symmetry properties (illustrated by the broken line), facilitating *9's-complement representation* useful in BCD subtraction.*

Coding to Detect Errors (Parity Checks)

Numerous codes have been developed to detect and even correct errors that occur in the data along its various transmission paths in the computer and between the computer and its peripheral devices. All such codes involve additional check bits that help to detect errors and sometimes also to pinpoint the erroneous bit or bits. We are concerned here only with the simplest and most widely used error-detection codes, namely *parity checks*. A parity check improves the reliability of data transmission by the addition of one extra bit to the coded information. There are two types of parity checks: the *odd parity* and the *even parity*. For the odd parity check the added check bit, p, has a value such that

$$p \oplus X_n \oplus X_{n-1} \oplus \cdots \oplus X_1 \oplus X_0 = 1, \tag{5.12}$$

* A detailed discussion on coding can be found in reference 1.

where the symbol $\oplus$ denotes *modulo-2 sum*: $1 \oplus 0 = 0 \oplus 1 = 1$, $1 \oplus 1 = 0$, $1 \oplus 1 \oplus 1 = 1$, and so on. In the even parity check the check bit p is chosen such that

$$p \oplus X_n \oplus X_{n-1} \oplus \cdots \oplus X_1 \oplus X_0 = 0. \qquad (5.13)$$

Example 5.12. The odd and even parity check bits for 10 BCD numbers are shown in Table 5.4.

Table 5.4 Odd and Even Parity Checks

Decimal Number	BCD Code 8 4 2 1	Parity Check Bit	
		Odd Parity	Even Parity
0	0 0 0 0	1	0
1	0 0 0 1	0	1
2	0 0 1 0	0	1
3	0 0 1 1	1	0
4	0 1 0 0	0	1
5	0 1 0 1	1	0
6	0 1 1 0	1	0
7	0 1 1 1	0	1
8	1 0 0 0	0	1
9	1 0 0 1	1	0

Note that both the odd and the even parity checks detect only an odd number of errors. However, the probability of double, quadruple, and so on, errors is negligible when the single error rate is low. Nevertheless, more sophisticated error-detection codes have also been developed to take care of noise bursts during transmission which may be the source of multiple errors; these are not discussed here.

Coding of Characters and Other Symbols (ASCII Codes)

Several codes have been developed to represent in binary form characters of the alphabet and additional symbols that are commonly available on the keyboards of peripheral devices. One such code that has attained widespread use in microcomputer systems is the *ASCII code;* ASCII is an acronym for American Standard Code for Information Interchange.

The full ASCII code requires 8 bits, hence 256 characters and symbols, including uppercase and lowercase letters, may be represented. Since many microcomputers have word lengths that are multiples of 4 bits, the most prevalent ASCII code is the 8-bit code. However, 6-bit and 7-bit "trimmed" ACSII codes have also been developed and may be used at the expense of some inconvenient "packing," that is, suitable programming.

5.4. FLOATING-POINT REPRESENTATION AND FLOATING-POINT ARITHMETIC

Floating-Point Representation

The *floating-point representation* of numbers, which is similar to the scientific notation, is important for the retention of maximum accuracy when operating with large or small numbers. It involves two quantities: the *exponent E* also called the *characteristic,* and the *mantissa M* also referred to as *fraction field.*

> **Example 5.13.** The speed of light is 300,000,000 meters/second. This may be expressed in scientific notation as 0.3×10^9 meters/second, and in floating-point representation by an exponent 9 and a mantissa 0.3.

The number of words required to express E and M is determined by the desired accuracy and by the word length of the microcomputer. The mantissa M is chosen such that

$$\tfrac{1}{2} \le |M| < 1. \tag{5.14}$$

Both the exponent and the mantissa may be expressed in 2's-complement representation, and the value of the mantissa M must be *normalized* to satisfy eq. 5.14.

> **Example 5.14.** To express $0.0074_8 = 0.000000111100_2$ in floating-point representation, we note that M does not satisfy eq. 5.14, hence must be normalized. Normalization may be performed by shifting the binary number into the range given by eq. 5.14; in this example this is attained by 6 shifts to the left. Hence 0.0074_8 in floating-point representation is expressed by an

exponent $E = 1\ 1010$ and by a mantissa $M = 0\ 1111$, where E is in 2's-complement representation and the trailing zeros in M have been omitted.

A floating-point representation that uses four 8-bit words is shown in Figure 5.2. The exponent is expressed by 7 bits of the first word in an "excess-64" notation in which 64_{10} is added to the exponent in order to accommodate positive and negative exponents without using a sign bit. The most significant bit of the first word is utilized as the sign bit of the mantissa and the remaining 24 bits of the mantissa are contained in the second, third, and fourth word. The range of numbers, N, that can be represented by the four words of Figure 5.2 can be shown to be (see also Problem 10):

$$2^{-65} \leq N \leq (1 - 2^{-24}) \cdot 2^{63}. \tag{5.15}$$

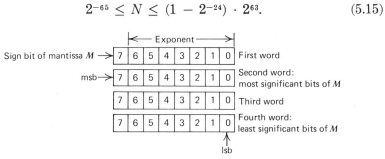

Figure 5.2. Floating-point representation using four 8-bit words.

Floating-Point Arithmetic

In adding or subtracting two numbers expressed in floating-point representation, the two numbers are first *aligned*, so that the exponent of the number with the larger magnitude becomes the exponent of the result.

For multiplication, the exponents are added while the mantissas are multiplied. Thus

$$X \cdot Y = (2^{E_X + E_Y}) \cdot (M_X \cdot M_Y). \tag{5.16}$$

Division of numbers in floating-point representation is performed by subtracting the exponents and dividing the mantissas:

$$X \div Y = (2^{E_X - F_Y}) \cdot (M_X \div M_Y). \tag{5.17}$$

The result of an arithmetic operation involving numbers in floating-point representation also requires normalization if M of the result is outside the range given in eq. 5.14.

PROBLEMS

1. Convert to decimal the following binary numbers: 101101, 0.101110, 110.101.

2. Determine the binary equivalent of the following decimal numbers: 123, 0.28125, 224.375.

3. Write eq. 5.3 in a general form that is applicable to any base b.

4. Compare equations 5.1 and 5.4 and establish the validity of the double-dabble algorithm for binary-to-decimal conversion.

5. The following binary numbers are given: 1 1010.01, 0 1010.01, 1 110010, 0 110010, 1 0100.11, 0 0100.11. Use eqs. 5.5 through 5.8 to find their decimal equivalents if the numbers are (a) in sign-and-magnitude representation, (b) in 1's-complement representation, and (c) in 2's-complement representation.

6. Express the following numbers in binary sign-and-magnitude representation, in 1's-complement representation, and 2's-complement representation: -1001.5_{10}, -853_{10}, -0.153_{10}, -52.0625_{10}. The round-off error should be smaller that the least significant digit given.

7. Express the following numbers in 8-4-2-1 BCD sign-and-magnitude representation: -93.2_{10}, -107.25_{10}, -0.769_{10}.

8. Establish algorithms for addition and subtraction using the excess-3 BCD code. Consider the corrections to be applied when (a) the result of an addition is less than 10_{10} in the code under consideration, (b) a carry to the next BCD digit is generated in an addition, (c) the result of a subtraction is less than 10_{10}, and (d) a borrow from the next BCD digit is generated in a subtraction.

9. Express the following numbers in floating-point representation: $+364_8$, -27.3_8, $+0A.04_{16}$, -0.025_{16}.

10. Verify eq. 5.15. *Hint:* the smallest value of $|M|$ is 2^{-1} and the largest value of $|M|$ is $(2^{24}-1) \cdot 2^{-24}$.

11. Discuss the shifting that is required for carrying out the addition of two numbers in floating-point representation when one number has a positive exponent and the other number a negative exponent.

12. Use floating-point binary representation and calculate $763.2_{10} -0.421_{10}$.

6

Arithmetic and Logic Circuits

Arithmetic and logic operations in a microcomputer are performed by *arithmetic* and *logic circuits*. Of these, the circuits for logic operations, addition, and subtraction are usually combined as an *arithmetic-logic unit* (ALU). This chapter provides details on *binary adders* and *subtractors*, *BCD adders*, and logic functions of the ALU, as well as brief descriptions of the accumulator and of *multiplier* and *divider circuits*.

6.1. ADDERS AND SUBTRACTORS

Binary Adders

In a microcomputer, two numbers are added by obtaining the augend from the accumulator (register A) and the addend from another register or from the main memory and adding them in an adder circuit. The result is placed in the accumulator, erasing its previous contents. Successive additions can also be carried out in this way, the accumulator assuming the new sum after each operation. An adder also incorporates an *overflow flip-flop* (or *flag*) *and/or a carry flag* (also known as link *flip-flop*) that is an extension bit of the accumulator. In any case, whenever an overflow flag or a carry flag is set it is only recognized by the CPU but no automatic action is taken. It is the responsibility of the programmer to test the state of the flag, to act upon it, and to clear the flag for future use.

45

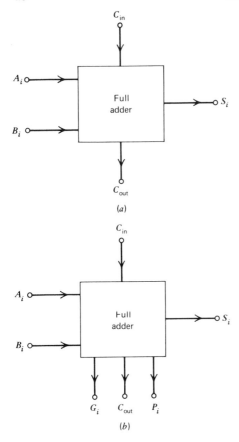

(a)

(b)

Figure 6.1. Full adders. (a) With carry-in C_{in} and carry-out C_{out}, (b) With carries C_{in} and C_{out} and with look-ahead carry outputs G_i and P_i.

The basic circuit in an adder is the *full adder* shown in Figure 6.1a in which A_i and B_i are the bits of the augend and addend, respectively, S_i is the sum, C_{in} is the carry input, and C_{out} is the carry output. The full adder is capable of bit-by-bit *serial* addition and is also the basic building block for *parallel adders.*

The simplest parallel adder is the *ripple-adder* which is realized by cascading n full adders for the addition of two n-bit numbers. The carry-out signal, C_{out}, however, must propagate through n *stages*, which may cause a significant delay in obtaining the final result. A faster *look-ahead carry adder* or *simultaneous-carry adder* can be obtained at the expense of more complex circuitry. In this type of adder, shown in Figure 6.1b, two auxiliary signals G_i (*generate*) and P_i (*propagate*) are generated at each bit, where $G_i = A_i\,B_i$ and $P_i = A_i \oplus B_i = A_i\,\overline{B}_i + \overline{A}_i\,B_i$.* It can

* In this chapter the "+" sign designates logical OR.

be shown (reference 1) that the carry inputs and the carry outputs in a
4-bit look-ahead carry adder are given by the equations

$$C_{in_0} = 0, \tag{6.1a}$$

$$C_{in_1} = G_0, \tag{6.1b}$$

$$C_{in_2} = G_1 + G_0 P_1, \tag{6.1c}$$

$$C_{in_3} = G_2 + G_1 P_2 + G_0 P_1 P_2, \tag{6.1d}$$

$$C_{out} = G_3 + G_2 P_3 + G_1 P_2 P_3 + G_0 P_1 P_2 P_3. \tag{6.1e}$$

Note that the propagation delay time of the carry output C_{out} in a
look-ahead carry adder is shorter than in a ripple-adder, since C_{out} need
not propagate through four full adders but only through two levels of
logic circuitry. A 4-bit look-ahead carry adder is outlined in Figure 6.2.
A total of n such adders may be cascaded to obtain a *hybrid adder* of
$4n$ bits.

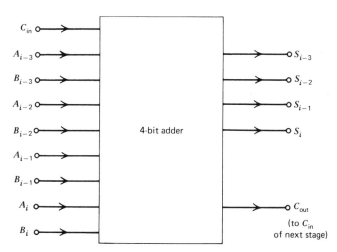

Figure 6.2. Four-bit look-ahead carry adder consisting of four circuits of
Figure 6.1b and of logic circuits that supply the carries according to eqs. 6.1.

Binary Subtractors

Since negative numbers can be expressed in three different representations, there are at least three types of subtractors: *sign-and-magnitude
subtractors, 1's-complement subtractors,* and *2's-complement subtractors.*

Sign-and-Magnitude Subtractors. These use the full subtractor—which is similar to the full adder—as their basic building block; *look-ahead borrow subtractors* can be also constructed like look-ahead carry adders. When performing the subtraction $A - B$ we must first establish which of the two numbers A and B has the larger magnitude; the result will have the sign of this number. The magnitude of the result is obtained as $A - B$ when $A > B$ and as $B - A$ when $A < B$.

1's-Complement Subtractors. In this representation the difference $A - B$ may be obtained as $-(B - A)$ by using a full adder and adding the 1's complement of the minuend A to the subtrahend B. However, in such a circuit a correction is required when $A - B$ is negative; the correction may be obtained by using an *end-around carry* from C_{out} to C_{in} as shown in Figure 6.3.

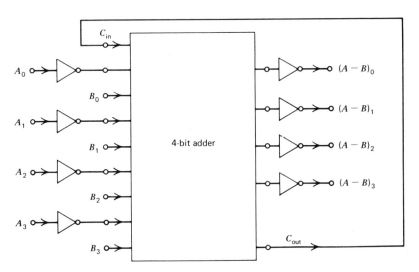

Figure 6.3. 1's-complement subtractor using the 4-bit adder of Figure 6.2 and an end-around carry.

Example 6.1. The difference $A - B$ for $A = 35_8$ and $B = 57_8$ may be obtained using the circuit of Figure 6.3 as follows: $A - B = -(B - A)$, thus we can write

$$B = 57_8 = \quad 0 \ 101111$$
$$-A = -35_8 = \quad 1 \ 100010 \leftarrow \text{1's complement of } A$$
$$\underline{}$$
$$1| 0 \ 010001 \leftarrow \text{uncorrected sum}$$
$$1 \leftarrow \text{end-around carry}$$
$$B - A \quad = \quad 0 \ 010010 \leftarrow \text{end-around carry added to un-corrected sum}$$
$$A - B \quad = \quad 1 \ 101101 \leftarrow \text{1's-complement representation of } (A - B)$$

2's-Complement Subtractors. In this representation the 2's complement of the subtrahend is first generated and is then added to the minuend. Thus the following operations are performed: inversion of all bits of the subtrahend by use of inverters; adding 1 to the result to obtain the 2's complement of the subtrahend; adding the minuend to the 2's complement of the subtrahend.

Binary-Coded Decimal Adders

In some microcomputers, particularly in calculators, arithmetic operations are carried out in binary-coded decimal (BCD) mostly in 8-4-2-1 BCD. While bit operations within a decimal digit are handled in parallel, digits are often handled serially.

The addition of two BCD numbers requires two 4-bit registers, and we assume here these to be the accumulator (register A) and register B. The least significant digits of the addend and the augend are presented first for addition, producing the least significant sum digit and possibly also a carry output. The resulting sum digit is entered into the accumulator at a clock pulse while the resulting carry is delayed by one clock period and is then added to the next sum digit. The contents of the accumulator and register B are shifted to the right at the addition of each pair of digits until all digits have been processed. Figure 6.4 illustrates the first three steps in the addition of the two 4-digit BCD numbers 64,327 and 2189.

A BCD adder for the addition of two BCD numbers must consider the following three situations that may arise in the 8-4-2-1 BCD code: (1) the sum of two digits, S, is such that $0000 \leq S \leq 1001$, so that the result is correct; (2) $1010 \leq S \leq 1111$, in which case the result is a nonvalid BCD combination, so that the BCD adder must make a correction; and

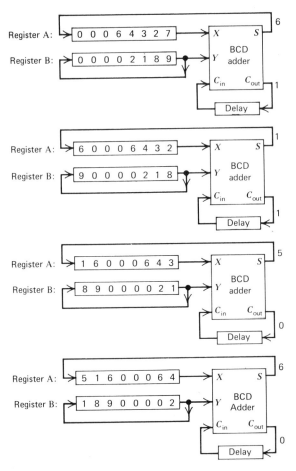

Figure 6.4. Three steps in the addition of the two BCD numbers $64{,}327_{10}$ and 2189_{10}. Each BCD adder block contains a 4-bit binary full adder and a correction circuit (see text).

(3) $10000 \le S \le 11001$ in which case a carry is generated and the result—as read in the given BCD code—is incorrect. Thus a correction is required in some cases and none in others. A combinational correction circuit in the BCD adder examines the BCD code of sum S and adds a 6_{10} to it when conditions (2) or (3) occur.

Example 6.2. This example shows the results of three BCD additions, conditions that require corrections, and the applied corrections.

(1) 5_{10} = 0101
    3_{10} = 0011

    sum = 1000 = 8_{10} (correct result)

(2) 6_{10} = 0110
    8_{10} = 1000

    (sum=)   1110 (nonvalid BCD number)
           0110 (add 6_{10})

    sum = 1 0100 = 14_{10} (correct BCD result)

(3) 9_{10} = 1001
    8_{10} = 1000

    (sum=) 1 0001 (a carry is generated and the result is in-
                   correct)
          0110 (add 6_{10})

    sum= 1 0111 = 17_{10} (correct BCD result)

6.2. MULTIPLIERS AND DIVIDERS

Circuits for these arithmetic operations usually are not incorporated in the CPU of a microcomputer. However, manufacturers often supply library subroutines for multiplication that are based on the pencil-and-paper method.

Although subroutines are adequate in many applications, some real-time control applications require faster techniques. One of these uses a 4×2 combinational multiplier (built on a single semiconductor chip) that generates partial products. Several such units are suitably connected for longer word lengths. The total multiplication time equals the maximum propagation delay of the partial products: in one circuit multiplication of two 16-bit numbers is performed in about 600 nanoseconds.

A somewhat slower technique utilizes ROMs as *look-up table* multipliers.

> **Example 6.3.** A ROM multiplier for two 4-bit words has $(2^4)^2 = 256$ output combinations of up to 8 bits. Thus the required number of ROM bits is $256 \times 8 = 2048$.

Multiplying two 8-bit words, however, would already require $(2^8)^2 \times 16 \approx 1$ million bits, which is impractical at present. The situation is substantially alleviated by employing more sophisticated techniques and by using several adders, thus considerably reducing the required number of ROM bits (reference 1).

As is the case for multiplication, division is also commonly supplied as a library subroutine by the manufacturer. Combinational dividers and ROM dividers are also possible for short word lengths.

6.3. THE ACCUMULATOR AND THE ARITHMETIC-LOGIC UNIT

The accumulator (register A) occupies an important position in the CPU, since all data to be operated upon must pass through it. It is often realized by a shift register with a number of bits equal to the word length of the microcomputer, and with parallel-in/parallel-out capabilities (reference 1).

The contents of the accumulator can be rotated or shifted right or left, and these operations may involve the carry bit if thus specified. The various possibilities are illustrated in Figure 6.5.

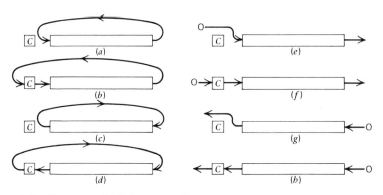

Figure 6.5. Rotate and shift accumulator operations. (*a*) Rotate right without carry, (*b*) rotate right with carry, (*c*) rotate left without carry, (*d*) rotate left with carry, (*e*) shift right without carry, (*f*) shift right with carry, (*g*) shift left without carry, and (*h*) shift left with carry.

In addition to the rotate and shift operations shown in Figure 6.5, a microcomputer may also provide *arithmetic rotate* and *arithmetic shift* operations. These operations are similar to the operations of Figure 6.5, except that they involve only the magnitude bits.

The structure and the functions of the ALU vary among microcomputers; a 4-bit ALU is outlined in Figure 6.6. It is similar to the 4-bit full adder with look-ahead carry and incorporates circuitry that enables it to

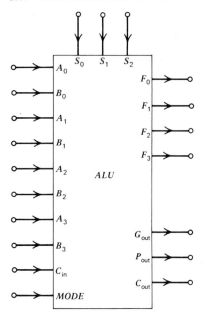

Figure 6.6. Block diagram of a 4-bit ALU.

Table 6.1 Function Table of a 4-Bit ALU

Function Select Inputs $S_2S_1S_0$	MODE = 1: Logic Operation F	MODE = 0: Arithmetic Operation F
0 0 0	$A + B$	A plus B
0 0 1	$A \cdot B$	Minus 1 (2's-complement)
0 1 0	$A \oplus B$	A minus 1
0 1 1	$A \odot B$	A plus $(A + B)$
1 0 0	0	A times 2
1 0 1	1	A plus $(A \cdot B)$
1 1 0	B	A minus B minus 1
1 1 1	A	A

Note: Symbols "$+$," "$\cdot$," "$\oplus$," and "$\odot$" refer to the logical OR, AND, EXCLUSIVE-OR, and COINCIDENCE operations, respectively; "plus," "minus," and "times" refer to arithmetic operations.

perform a number of arithmetic and logic operations, as shown in Table 6.1. The MODE binary level determines whether a logic operation or an arithmetic operation is to be performed, while the *function select* inputs S_2, S_1, and S_0 determine the specific logic or arithmetic function.

Logic operations are performed bit by bit and include the AND and the OR operations, as well as the EXCLUSIVE-OR operation $A \oplus B = A\overline{B} + \overline{A}B$, and the EQUALITY (or COINCIDENCE) operation $A \odot B = AB + \overline{A}\overline{B}$. Arithmetic operations include the plus, minus, times 2, and combinations of the plus operation with the logical AND and OR operations.

Several ALUs of Figure 6.6 may be cascaded for word lengths longer than 4 bits ("*bit slicing*"). In such applications carry propagation is facilitated by the C_{in}, C_{out}, G_{out}, and P_{out} connections.

PROBLEMS

1. Use 2's-complement representation and show examples of addition with arithmetic overflow.

2. Use 2's-complement representation and show examples of addition in which the carry flag is set.

3. Utilize eqs. 6.1 and draw a logic diagram of a 4-bit adder with look-ahead carry.

4. Utilize the 4-bit adder of Figure 6.2 and draw a block diagram of a 16-bit hybrid adder. Discuss the total propagation delay time.

5. Complete the BCD addition of Figure 6.4.

6. Draw a truth table and demonstrate the requirement for a correction in the addition of two BCD numbers having a sum $> 1001_2 = 9_{10}$.

7. Describe the arithmetic shift right and shift left operations that are required for the normalization of floating-point numbers in arithmetic operations.

7

The Main Memory

This chapter describes the elements, organization, and operation of the *main memory* of the microcomputer. Although in principle the main memory could include any storage media that can be organized to perform a memory function, the discussion here focuses on *semiconductor memories* widely used in microcomputers.

7.1. SEMICONDUCTOR MEMORIES

Semiconductor memories are cellular arrays of semiconductor storage elements, or *cells*, that contain binary information. Typically 256 to 16,384 identical cells are included on a single semiconductor chip. Semiconductor memories can be classified according to application, manufacturing technology, or operating speed.

Application of Memories

The two most commonly used semiconductor memories are the *random-access memory* (RAM) which is of the *read-and-write* type, and the *read-only memory* (ROM) used for storing fixed information such as programs, subroutines, and look-up tables. Both the RAM and the ROM are arrays of memory cells; a ROM, however, cannot be written into during operation, since information determining the binary value (0 or 1) of each bit can be inserted only during fabrication.

In developing a program, field-programming facilities that enable the user to insert the information in the ROM are often desirable. This requirement prompted the development of the *programmable ROM*, or *pROM*. There are two basic methods of field programming. In one method each cell in the array incorporates a metallic link that may be fused during programming by the application of a high-current pulse of specified duration. A broken link in a cell defines one binary value, and an unbroken link represents the other binary value. Alternatively, a memory array consists of cells that are programmed by selectively establishing a short-circuit by means of avalanche breakdown.

In a pROM, the structure of a cell is irreversibly altered for one of the two binary values, 0 or 1. The additional flexibility of reversing such previous decisions is provided by *reprogrammable ROMs*. In one such reprogrammable ROM information is inserted via an avalanche process. Information may be erased by application of ultraviolet light through a quartz window which allows reprogramming. This sequence may be repeated several times without affecting performance.

Memory Technologies

Memory cells may be fabricated from metal-oxide-silicon field-effect transistors (MOSFETs) or from bipolar transistors. The number of transistors required for one memory cell has diminished with developmental effort from 8 to 1; a 3-transistor configuration is described in detail here. The cell is of the *dynamic* type: it has no positive feedback between the active components for latching the information into a stable state, but the information is stored on the stray capacitance of a FET electrode.

The operation of a 3-transistor n-channel MOS memory cell is discussed with reference to Figure 7.1. The cell consists of transistors Q_1, Q_2, and Q_3, and of capacitance C_G. Transistor Q_4 is common to all memory cells in a *column* of the array and serves to *precharge* capacitance C_D. To read the contents of the memory cell, C_D is initially precharged to a voltage near V_{DD} and the *READ SELECT* line, which is common to a *row* of a cell array, is to logic "1", that is, to $V_{DD} = +12$ volts. If the voltage across C_G is initially above the threshold voltage of Q_2, C_D is discharged via Q_2 and Q_3; conversely, C_D remains charged to a voltage near V_{DD} if the voltage across C_G is initially below the threshold voltage of Q_2. Hence the complement of the binary information on C_G is transferred to capacitance C_D on the *READ DATA* line without altering the state of C_G. Writing into the cell is performed by setting to logic "1" the *WRITE SELECT* line, which is common to a row of a cell array. This turns Q_1 on and transfers to capacitance C_G the state of the *WRITE DATA* line, which is common to a column of a cell array.

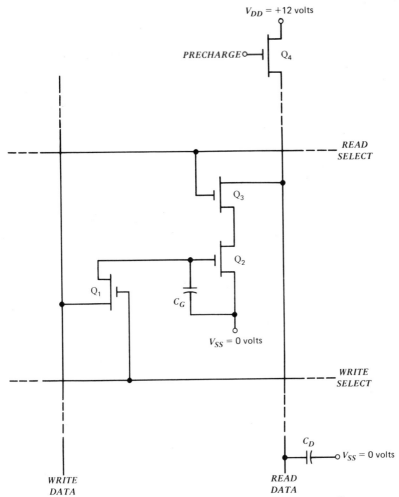

Figure 7.1. A 3-transistor *n*-channel MOS dynamic memory cell.

Although readout is not destructive, the charge on capacitance C_G deteriorates because of leakage, requiring that information be periodically written into each cell of the memory even when the content of a cell remains unchanged. This is performed by periodic *refreshing* that consists of reading the content of a cell and rewriting the data back into the same cell. Circuits performing this task are discussed in Section 7.5.

Bipolar memories are commonly of the static type, that is, two inverters are connected in a positive feedback configuration to attain two stable states. A bipolar memory cell using triple-emitter transistors for word selection and data gating is shown in Figure 7.2. For writing or reading operations both the *COLUMN SELECT* and the *ROW SELECT* lines have to be raised in coincidence. During a write operation information is inserted into the cell by forcing the Q or the $\bar{Q}$ line to the low binary state; for reading, the current flowing in these lines is sensed.

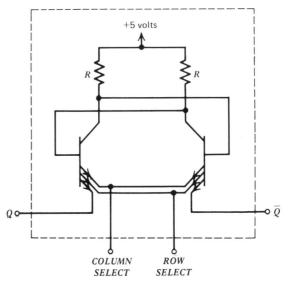

Figure 7.2. A triple-emitter bipolar memory cell with coincidence addressing.

The use of the triple-emitter memory cell of Figure 7.2 is illustrated in Figure 7.3 for an array consisting of 16 bits. It includes address inputs A_0 through A_3, as well as a *CHIP SELECT* (*CS*) input that enables the array and facilitates the use of several arrays in a memory. The *READ* "0" and *READ* "1" outputs of the 3-state type are enabled by a common *READ ENABLE* signal permitting parallel connections with similar outputs of other arrays.

Operating Speeds

The operating speed of a memory may be expressed by several parameters. One of these is the *access time*, which is the time elapsed from the application of a memory address to a valid output from the memory. It is typically in the range of several nanoseconds to 2 microseconds and depends on the technology and the number of words in the memory. Another parameter is the *cycle time*, which is the minimum time

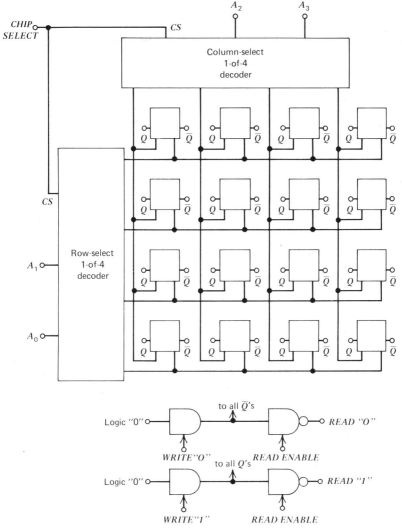

Figure 7.3. Block diagram of a 16-bit RAM array with coincidence addressing. Each bit uses one cell of **Figure 7.2.**

required between the initiation of successive *memory read, memory write,* or *memory read-modify-write* operations.

In general, MOS memories are slower than bipolar memories; the shortest access times attainable in bipolar memories are in the vicinity of 5 nanoseconds.

7.2. MEMORY ORGANIZATION

The organization of a bipolar RAM using a triple-emitter memory cell was shown in Figure 7.3. When the higher operating speed of the bipolar circuit is not required, higher-density MOS circuits may be used. A block diagram of a 4096-bit MOS RAM is shown in Figure 7.4. Each bit in the RAM is individually addressable (*bit organization*). The 12-bit address $A_{11} - A_0$ is decoded by the *row* and *column decoders* to 2×64 lines, and a bit is selected by a coincidence between an output line of the row decoder and an output line of the column decoder.

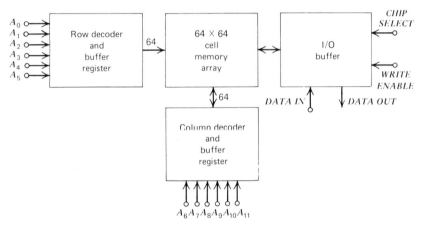

Figure 7.4. Simplified block diagram of a 4096 words × 1-bit MOS RAM.

While bit organization is prevalent in larger RAMs, *word organization* is used primarily in smaller RAMs and in ROMs. In a word organized memory, an *address decoder* selects a word with a word length of several, rather than a single, bit.

7.3. SHIFT REGISTERS

In addition to the memory types discussed thus far, a microcomputer may also utilize *shift registers*. A shift register consists of a linear array of storage elements: information in the array is shifted by the application of a *shift clock* (which is typically a 2-phase or a 4-phase clock), and the direction of the shifting is fixed or is determined by the *shift direction* control. Information can be entered and removed at the ends of the linear array; in some shift registers it is also possible to enter or delete information at additional points along the array.

Because of their iterative structure combined with high component density, shift registers provide an inexpensive medium for information storage, and capacities of 2×1024 bits on a single semiconductor chip are readily available.* Another type of shift register is the *charge-coupled device* (CCD) that is available up to 16,384 bits on one semiconductor chip.

7.4. AUXILIARY REGISTERS

In addition to the memory elements described above, orderly flow of information to and from the main memory also requires several auxiliary registers as well as data and address buses. A block diagram that includes several auxiliary registers is shown in Figure 7.5. The *memory data*

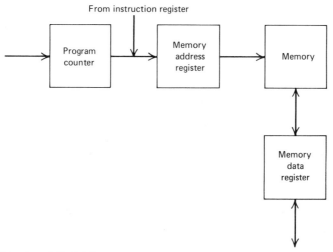

Figure 7.5. Simplified block diagram of a memory showing the program counter, the memory address register, and the memory data register.

register (MDR) is instrumental in transferring the data to and from the main memory. The *memory address register* (MAR) has the capacity to uniquely address each word in the main memory; its information is derived from the *instruction register*, or from the *program counter* that contains the address of the next instruction to be fetched and usually is incremented after this address has been transferred to the MAR.

---

* A detailed description of the operation of shift registers is given in reference 1.

7.5. REFRESH CIRCUITS FOR DYNAMIC MOS RAMs

We saw in Figure 7.1 that the information in a dynamic MOS memory cell is retained on a small capacitance—which is typically much less than 1 picofarad. Such volatile storage is subject to destruction of information, especially at elevated temperatures since leakage currents double for each increase of about 10°C in temperature. Thus some means must be found to return the capacitor to its original charge state. Specifications for maximum allowed intervals between such refresh operations are conservative and call for a refresh once every few milliseconds.

An illustration of a refresh circuit for a memory organized around a 4096 word × 1 bit MOS RAM chip is shown in Figure 7.6. The 4096 bits are arranged in $2^6 = 64$ rows and in 64 columns. Since it is commonly required to apply the refresh signals only to the rows of a RAM, the refresh operation is sequenced by a 6-bit *refresh counter*. A refresh operation is initiated by the *refresh timer* once every 30 microsecond; this way every one of the 64 rows is refreshed at regular intervals of about 2

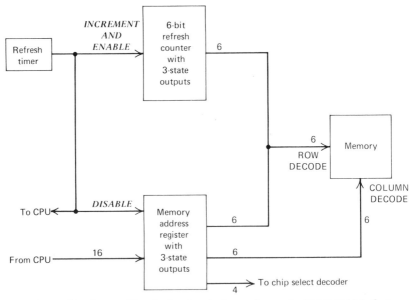

Figure 7.6. "Cycle steal" refresh circuit for a dynamic MOS RAM that uses 4096 words × 1-bit memory arrays. Note that the address and the data lines of the CPU must be disabled during refresh.

milliseconds. A refresh cycle (*"cycle steal"*) disables the operation of the CPU (*"CPU freeze"*), sets into inactive (high impedance) states the outputs of the memory address register, increments the refresh counter, and activates the 3-state outputs of the refresh counter.

In some memory cell structures it is also possible to refresh by periodic application of a *single* refresh pulse that refreshes the whole memory.

7.6. ADDRESSING MODES

The length of an instruction in a microcomputer is in many cases adequate to include the full address of the specified memory location.

> **Example 7.1.** A microcomputer with an 8-bit word length has $2^{16} = 65,636$ memory locations. A "load accumulator" instruction consists of an 8-bit operator that designates the instruction; this is followed by a 16-bit operand that specifies the memory address from which data are to be loaded into the accumulator.

Some microcomputers, however, have a limited number of bits in their memory reference instruction formats which, therefore, do not permit the addressing of the whole memory. This has resulted in the development of various *addressing modes*. In most of these, an *effective address* is calculated by combining the instruction word address bits with another word that was previously entered into a register or into a specified memory location; hence two words are required to completely specify one memory location. In what follows, four of these addressing modes are illustrated with a 16-bit instruction word shown in Figure 7.7. The 6 most significant bits are reserved for the operator while the 8 least signifi-

Figure 7.7. Sixteen-bit instruction word of a microcomputer with four different addressing modes.

cant bits represent the *address field*, also called *displacement field*, that allows addressing of 256 memory words. Two additional bits, namely bits 8 and 9, designated *addressing mode bits*, provide the four addressing modes.

Base Page Addressing

Base page addressing is the simplest addressing mode; it is also known as *addressing on page 0*.

> **Example 7.2.** Assume that bits 8 and 9 of Figure 7.7 are 00, designating base page addressing. The range of memory words that may be addressed by this scheme lies between 0 and 255.

Addressing with a Page Register

The base page addressing scheme described above would suffice only for the smallest memory systems. To increase the addressing capacity as required by a larger memory, we set up a *page register*. As in base page addressing, each page consists of only 256 words. However, the page register allows the program to recognize which set of 256 words, that is, which *page* is to be used at any given step in memory referencing. In effect, the page register adds higher-order bits to the instruction address, thus permitting the addressing of additional memory locations as shown in Figure 7.8. Although an additional instruction is now required for page register setting, the scheme may be attractive if care is exercised by the programmer to effect the majority of memory referencing within the selected page.

> **Example 7.3.** Assume that bits 8 and 9 of Figure 7.7 are 01, designating addressing with a page register. The page register of Figure 7.8 is loaded with 10000001 ($= 129_{10}$) which are the higher-order bits of an effective 16-bit address; hence page 129_{10} is selected by the decoder. The addresses that can be accessed by including the 8 lower-order bits are thus in the range of 129×2^8 to $129 \times 2^8 + 255$, that is, $33,024_{10}$ to $33,279_{10}$.

Addressing Relative to the Program Counter

In this addressing mode the 8 least significant bits of the instruction word are treated as a signed binary number in which bit 7 takes on the

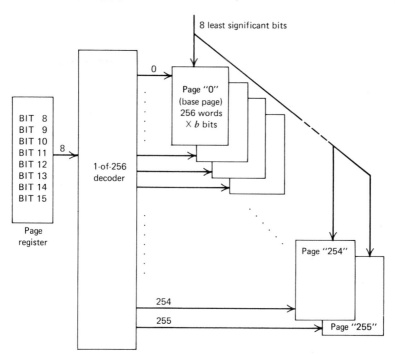

Figure 7.8. Addressing with a page register. Each of the 256 pages is selected via the auxiliary page register, and each page has a capacity of 256 words.

function of the sign. The effective address is obtained by adding the contents of the program counter, (PC), to the signed number thus formed. This permits relative addressing within the range of $(PC) - 128_{10}$ to $(PC) + 127_{10}$. If the program counter has already been incremented at the time the address is formed and is thus pointing to the next instruction, the addressing range is $(PC) - 127_{10}$ to $(PC) + 128_{10}$.

Base page addressing and addressing relative to the program counter are economical, since they do not require additional instructions for page setting. Although their addressing ranges are modest, careful programming may effect many memory reference instructions within their ranges. Also, addressing relative to the program counter simplifies program relocation, which aids in combining different program segments and resident (library) subroutines.

Addressing Relative to an Index Register

In this addressing mode the effective address is generated by the sum of the contents of an *index register* and the contents of the displacement field. The advantage of using index registers lies in their capability of being modified (i.e., cleared, loaded, incremented, or decremented) in a fraction of a memory cycle. Hence index modification is a convenient way to address different elements of arrays and other data structures.

7.6. INDIRECT ADDRESSING

Indirect addressing means that the address found by any of the addressing modes discussed so far does not itself contain the desired operand but only its address. Thus the memory reference instruction addresses a memory location whose contents serve only as a *pointer* to the desired address. Usually the instruction contains one bit that determines whether the addressing mode is direct or indirect.

Example 7.4. Indirect addressing is illustrated in Figure 7.9. Unlike in Figure 7.7, the instruction word consists of a 7-bit operator, a D/I bit designating direct or indirect addressing

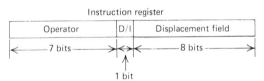

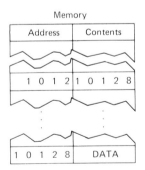

Figure 7.9. Illustration of indirect addressing.

mode, and an 8-bit displacement field. Figure 7.9 also shows portions of the main memory. We assume that the D/I bit of the instruction register indicates indirect addressing mode. Thus when address 1012 is referenced by the MAR, the contents of location 1012 are interpreted as the *address*, that is, location 10,128, where the next operand can be found.

PROBLEMS

1. How many 256 words × 1 bit RAM circuits are required for a memory system of 1024 words × 8 bits? Draw a block diagram of the system including address decoders for chip selection.

2. Given a 1024-bit serial recirculating shift register, such as discussed in Section 7.3, design a 1024 words × 8 bits recirculating memory. Show the additional digital circuits that are required to determine the bit position where information may be deleted or new data may be inserted.

3. Discuss the relative advantages of RAMs and shift registers and describe some applications for both memory types.

4. Discuss the relative merits of addressing with a page register and addressing relative to the program counter. Show an example of each.

5. In the addressing with a page register shown in Figure 7.8, the page register is set to 10100100 and the lower-order bits are 01011011. Which page will be selected and what memory location will be addressed?

8

The Control Unit

The control unit is the "nerve center" of the microcomputer. It provides sequencing and timing for the processing of instructions and controls the data paths between the various parts of the microcomputer.

8.1. SEQUENCING

An instruction in a microcomputer is performed in one or more *processor cycles,* also designated *machine cycles, microcycles,* or *basic instruction cycles.* A processor cycle consists of two principal *phases:* the *fetch* (or *addressing*) *phase* and the *execute phase.* Each fetch phase is utilized for addressing a memory location via the memory address register (MAR) and for transfering data between the memory data register (MDR) and the addressed location. In the case of some simple instructions, a complete instruction is fetched in a single fetch phase and is executed in a single execute phase.

> **Example 8.1.** In Example 2.3, addition was performed by adding the contents of register B to the contents of the accumulator and placing the result in the accumulator. The instruction for this addition occupies only one memory location, thus it can be fetched in a single fetch phase. Furthermore, since it involves only the CPU and does not require additional memory referencing, it can be executed in a single execute phase. As a result, the instruction is completed in a single fetch phase and a single execute phase, hence in a single processor cycle.

68

Instructions, especially in microcomputers that have word lengths of less than 16 bits, may occupy more than one memory location.

> **Example 8.2.** A microprocessor has a word length of 8 bits and a main memory that consists of $2^{16} = 65,536$ words. The storage of a jump instruction requires three memory locations: the first location contains the jump instruction code in machine language; the second and third locations contain the 16-bit address specifying the memory location to which the program should jump.

An instruction that occupies more than one memory location requires more than one fetch phase, hence more than one processor cycle. The execute phase of an instruction, however, usually cannot begin until the entire instruction has been transferred into the *instruction register*. For this reason, execute phases are idle in (or are omitted from) the processor cycles until all required fetch phases have been completed.

In many cases, as in Example 8.1, the fetched instruction does not require further memory referencing: such an instruction is executed during the execute phase following the fetch phase that completes the transfer of the instruction into the instruction register. When the execution of the fetched instruction requires further memory referencing, it incurs an additional processor cycle.

> **Example 8.3.** This example illustrates the sequencing of processor cycles and the use of fetch and execute phases in an add instruction. The microcomputer of the example has a word length of 8 bits and a main memory that consists of $2^{16} = 65,536$ words.
>
> Selected parts of the main memory are shown in Table 8.1. The instruction "Add the contents of memory location 1205 to the contents of the accumulator and place the result into the accumulator" is stored in memory locations 101, 102, and 103. Location (address) 101 contains the instruction code for the addition, which is 11000001 ($= C1_{16}$) in the machine language of the microcomputer. Location 102 contains the most significant 8 bits of the binary equivalent of 1205, location 103 the least significant 8 bits. Location 1205 contains the addend 00001111 $= 15_{10} = F_{16}$.
>
> Sequencing of the processor cycles and of the fetch and execute phases is shown in Figure 8.1. The contents of the accumu-

Table 8.1 Processing of the Add Instructions in Example 8.3: Selected Parts of the Main Memory

Address		Contents	
Decimal	Binary	Binary	Hexadecimal
0	0000000000000000	????????	??
1	0000000000000001	????????	??
.	.	.	.
.	.	.	.
.	.	.	.
101	0000000001100101	11000001	C1
102	0000000001100110	00000100	04
103	0000000001100111	10110101	B5
.	.	.	.
.	.	.	.
.	.	.	.
1205	0000010010110101	00001111	0F
.	.	.	.
.	.	.	.
.	.	.	.
65534	1111111111111110	????????	??
65535	1111111111111111	????????	??

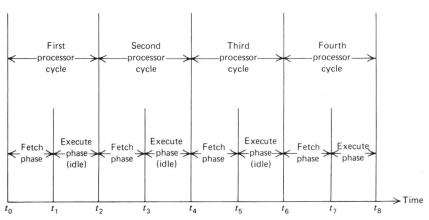

Figure 8.1. Processing of the add instruction in Example 8.3: sequencing of the processor cycles and of the fetch and execute phases.

Table 8.2 Processing of the Add Instruction in Example 8.3: Contents of the Accumulator, the MAR, the MDR, and the Instruction Register at Times t_0 through t_8

Processor Cycle	Phase	Time	Accumulator		MAR		MDR		Instruction Register	
			Binary	Decimal	Binary	Decimal	Binary	Hexadecimal	Binary	Hexadecimal
1	Fetch	t_0	00011000	24	0000000001100101	101	???????	??	????????????????????	??????
	Execute	t_1	00011000	24	0000000001100101	101	11000001	C1	11000001?????????????????	C1????
2	Fetch	t_2	00011000	24	0000000001100110	102	11000001	C1	11000001???????????????	C1????
	Execute	t_3	00011000	24	0000000001100110	102	00000100	04	1100000100000100???????	C104??
3	Fetch	t_4	00011000	24	0000000001100111	103	00000100	04	1100000100000100???????	C104??
	Execute	t_5	00011000	24	0000000001100111	103	10110101	B5	110000010000010010110101	C104B5
4	Fetch	t_6	00011000	24	0000010010110101	1205	10110101	B5	110000010000010010110101	C104B5
	Execute	t_7	00011000	24	0000010010110101	1205	00001111	0F	110000010000010010110101	C104B5
	Execute	t_8	00100111	39	????????????????	????	00001111	0F	110000010000010010110101	C104B5

71

lator, the memory address register, the memory data register, and the instruction register during the processing of the instruction are shown in Table 8.2.

During the fetch phase of the first processor cycle, that is t_0 to t_1, memory location 101 is addressed via the 16-bit MAR and the instruction code $11000001 = C1_{16}$ is fetched from that location into the first 8 bits of the instruction register via the MDR. These 8 bits indicate that the instruction is not complete, and as a result the execute phase in the first processor cycle (t_1 to t_2) is idle.

During the fetch phase of the second processor cycle (t_2 to t_3), the most significant 8 bits of the address 1205 are fetched from memory location 102 into the second 8 bits of the instruction register. The instruction is still not complete, thus the execute phase in the second processor cycle (t_3 to t_4) is also idle.

During the fetch phase of the third processor cycle (t_4 to t_5), the least significant 8 bits of address 1205 are fetched from memory location 103 and they are deposited into the third 8 bits of the instruction register. Now the instruction in the instruction register is complete and it indicates that the contents of memory location 1205 have to be fetched. The execute phase of the third processor cycle (t_5 to t_6) is idle.

During the fetch phase of the fourth processor cycle, that is, t_6 to t_7, memory location 1205 is addressed via the 16-bit MAR and its contents are fetched into the MDR. The addition is executed during the execute phase (t_7 to t_8) by adding the contents of the MDR, which is 15, to the contents of the accumulator, which is 24, and placing the resulting 39 in the accumulator.

Memory referencing may involve the transfer of an instruction, part of an instruction, or data from the main memory to the MDR, as was the case in Example 8.3; conversely, memory referencing may also involve data transfer from the MDR to the main memory.

Example 8.4. A microcomputer has a word length of 8 bits and a main memory that consists of $2^{16} = 65,536$ words. The instruction "Store the contents of the accumulator in memory location 1305" is stored in memory addresses 201, 202, and 203. Location 201 contains the instruction code for store which is 00001101 in the machine language of the microcomputer. Location 202 contains the most significant 8 bits of the binary equivalent of 1305, location 203 the least significant 8 bits. The contents of the accumulator are $11000011 = 195_{10}$.

The contents of memory location 1305 are not known initially: the store instruction will transfer the number 195_{10} from the accumulator to memory location 1305 via the MDR, destroying the previous contents of location 1305 in the process. The contents of the accumulator remain unchanged, that is, 195_{10}.

Transfer of data from the MDR to the main memory takes place during a fetch (addressing) phase, even when—as in Example 8.4—the transfer is part of the execution of an instruction.

Example 8.5. The sequencing of the store instruction of Example 8.4 is illustrated in Figure 8.2. The instruction is fetched during the first three fetch phases. The execution of the instruction, that is, the storage of the number 195_{10} in memory location 1305, is performed during the fourth fetch phase.

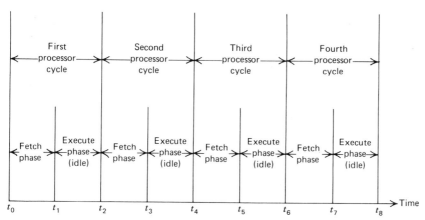

Figure 8.2. Sequencing of the processor cycles and of the fetch and execute phases in Example 8.5.

The fetch phase is frequently extended by the addition of an auxiliary *wait phase* (also known as *wait state*) when the *access time* of the addressed memory location exceeds the duration of the fetch phase. The duration of the wait phase is chosen long enough to assure the completion of data transfer between the MDR and the addressed memory location.

Another auxiliary phase is the *halt phase* (also known as *halt state*) that stops the operation of the CPU—but dynamic memories are kept refreshed when required. The halt phase, which is entered by inserting a halt instruction or a signal on a special halt line, is terminated either by an interrupt or by manual intervention via front panel controls.

8.2. TIMING

A processor cycle is divided into *time states* of identical durations. This duration is determined by the system clock, hence is fixed in a given microcomputer; it is typically between 0.1 and 3 microseconds. The number of time states may vary for an execute phase, a wait phase, or a halt phase. However, the number of time states in a fetch phase is usually constant in a microcomputer.

> **Example 8.6.** A microcomputer has a word length of 8 bits and a main memory consisting of $2^{16} = 65,536$ words. The addressing of the memory locations uses 16 bits that are sent from the CPU to the main memory via an 8-bit data bus during two sequential time states. Thus the fetch phase consists of two time states. However, it may be followed by a wait phase consisting of any number of time states.

8.3. DATA PATHS AND BUS STRUCTURE

Data flow between the various parts of a microcomputer takes place via interconnecting data paths. Data flow, which includes the flow of instructions as well, may be unidirectional, such as the transmission of an address from the MAR to the main memory, or bidirectional, such as between the MDR and the main memory. When the data path is unidirectional, it can be activated (enabled) by an AND gate in each bit of the path. When the data path is bidirectional, a direction control signal must be also supplied to a circuit similar to that of Figure 4.1.

The *bus structure* of a microcomputer is comprised of all the data paths. The operation of a bus is illustrated in the example that follows.

> **Example 8.7.** Data communication among three registers of a microcomputer with a word length of 4 bits is illustrated in

Figure 8.3. The outputs of the D-E flip-flops are connected to the data bus via logic circuits with 3-state outputs (see page 21), which are activated by the $SEND$ controls. The D inputs of the D-E flip-flops are also connected to the data bus and are activated by the $RECEIVE$ controls. A maximum of one $SEND$ control and any number of $RECEIVE$ controls may be activated at a given time. Figure 8.3 illustrates the operation of the data bus with three 4-bit registers; additional registers may be connected in parallel to the data bus.

During the processing of an instruction, the control unit activates the data paths that are required to fetch the instruction from the main memory into the instruction register. The instruction is decoded by the *instruction decoder* which determines what additional data paths are required.

Example 8.8.   In Example 8.3, the data paths required to fetch the first 8 bits of the instruction are activated at time t_0 (see Figure 8.1 and Table 8.2). These 8 bits are fetched and are decoded by the instruction decoder by time t_1. The 8 bits indicate that the processing of the instruction will require three additional fetch phases and an execute phase. Data paths for these phases will be activated at times t_2, t_4, t_6, and t_7, respectively.

8.4.   MICROPROGRAMMING

The data paths and their sequence of activation are governed by the instruction set of the microcomputer. Thus once an instruction set is selected and the instruction decoder and the required data paths are built into the *hardware* of the microcomputer, it is not possible to alter or expand the instruction set. A more flexible arrangement is provided by realizing the instruction decoder and the data path controls by *firmware* such as read-only memory (ROM): the result is a *microprogrammed* microcomputer. It should be noted that the word microprogramming is *not* an abbreviation of microcomputer programming, but describes a method for the activation of data paths.

In microprogramming, the data paths of a machine-language instruction are activated by a *microprogram*, the data paths of a processor cycle (microcycle) are activated by a *microinstruction*, and the data paths of a time state are activated by a *microoperation*. Thus a microprogram

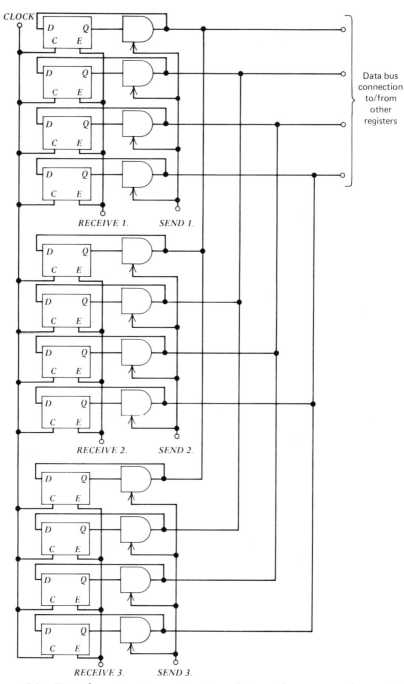

Figure 8.3. Data bus structure activating data paths among three 4-bit registers.

76

consists of one or more microinstructions, and a microinstruction consists of one or more microoperations.

In principle, each instruction in a microprogrammed microcomputer could be represented by a microprogram stored in a ROM. In reality, however, this approach would require an impractically large ROM. This situation may be alleviated by replacing the ROM with a more elaborate *programmable logic array* (PLA). In another approach, sequences of microoperations that occur in several microinstructions are stored only once in the form of a microprogrammed subroutine, or *microroutine*.

> **Example 8.9.** All processor cycles that require the transfer of a word from the main memory to the MDR utilize identical data paths for their fetch phases. The sequencing information for data path control of these fetch phases is stored in a microroutine.

The circuitry required by the microprogramming includes a ROM that is programmed (masked) for a particular instruction set. The ROM provides *data path control* that activates the required data paths, and *next address control* that determines the location of the next microoperation. Logic circuits external to the ROM include a *ROM address control* and a *ROM address register*.

8.5. BLOCK DIAGRAM OF A MICROCOMPUTER

A simplified block diagram that shows details of the CPU is given in Figure 8.4 for a hypothetical microcomputer. Note that the structure is somewhat arbitrary and varies widely among the various microcomputer types.

The word length is 8 bits, thus the ALU, the accumulator, register B, and the MDR all have 8-bit storage capacities. The 16-bit MAR can address $2^{16} = 65,536$ memory locations; the program counter and each of the 7 levels of the *address stack* (see Chapter 9) also have 16-bit capacities. The instruction register can store 24 bits: 8 bits for the operator and 16 bits for the operand. Data path control is performed by a microprogrammed ROM consisting of $2^7 = 128$ words of 30 bits each; auxiliary circuitry includes a ROM address control and a 7-bit ROM address register.

The CPU of the microcomputer communicates with the outside world via the I/O section which was described in detail in Chapter 4. Arithmetic and logic instructions are performed by the ALU, the accumulator, register B, and the 4 flags.

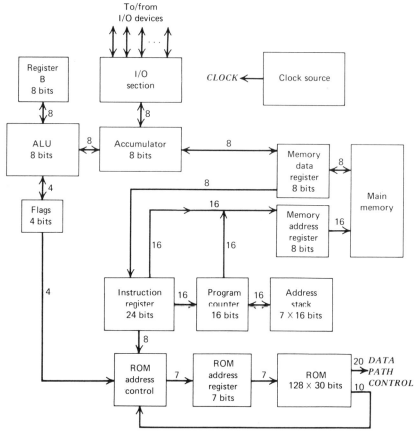

Figure 8.4. Simplified block diagram of a microcomputer.

Details of the main memory may be found in Chapter 7; it communicates data with the CPU via the bidirectional MDR and is addressed by the MAR, which may be loaded either from the program counter or from the operand field of the instruction register. Instructions are transferred from the main memory to the instruction register via the MDR in three 8-bit *bytes*.

Instructions are executed by the ROM, governed by the ROM address control which combines information from the flags, the operator field of the instruction register, and the next address control of the ROM. Data paths, as well as internal operations of the ALU and the I/O section, are controlled by the data path control of the ROM.

PROBLEMS

1. Which instructions of Section 3.1 can be performed in a single processor cycle?

2. Replace the question marks at t_0 and t_8 in Table 8.2 by appropriate 1's and 0's for the case when the instruction is preceded and followed by an identical instruction.

3. How will Table 8.2 change if memory location 1205 contains 21 instead of 15?

4. Prepare a table that shows the relevant locations of the main memory preceding and following the processing of the instruction described in Examples 8.4 and 8.5.

5. Prepare a table that shows the contents of the accumulator, MAR, MDR, and instruction register at time t_0 through t_8 in the instruction described in Examples 8.4 and 8.5.

6. Is a wait phase required in the microcomputer of Example 8.6 if the memory access time equals the duration of (a) 0.5 time state, (b) 2.5 time states?

7. Find the time required for the instruction processing described in Example 8.3 if the duration of a fetch phase and of an execute phase is 1 microsecond, and if the memory access time is less than 1 microsecond. Repeat for the case when the unnecessary execute phases are omitted.

8. Establish the binary values of the *RECEIVE* and *SEND* signals that are required in Figure 8.3 to load the contents of the uppermost 4-bit register into both other registers. Assume that a binary 1 is required for activation.

9. Describe all data paths that are activated during the processing of the add instruction in Example 8.3.

10. List those fetch and execute phases in the instructions of Section 3.1 that would be realized by microroutines in a microprogrammed microcomputer.

9

Additional Features

This chapter presents software features that are more advanced than those discussed in Chapter 3. They include descriptions of assemblers, loaders, data structures, subroutine linkages, simulators, and operating systems. Hardware features associated with system operation are also examined.

9.1. ASSEMBLERS

An *assembler,* or *symbolic assembler,* program translates a program from an assembly language into a machine language. It also assigns memory locations to instructions, variables, and constants. Each assembly-language instruction is translated into one machine-language instruction with the exceptions of macroinstructions (see p. 14), and of *pseudoinstructions.* Pseudoinstructions include assignment of specific values (e.g., EQUATE $W = 1.5$), definition of macroinstructions (e.g., DEFINE MACRO MAC1), specification of I/O ports, various start and end instructions, specifications for the storage of blocks of data, and format specifications.

The operation of the assembler is illustrated by a program based on the statement from Example 3.7: "IF $V > W$ THEN $X \leftarrow Y - 1$ ELSE $X \leftarrow Y + 1$." A flow chart of the program is shown in Figure 9.1 and an assembly-language program in Table 9.1. With the exception of pseudoinstructions EQUATE and END, each instruction is numbered by a *line number.* These line numbers are not utilized by the assembler but are provided for the aid of the programmer. Each numbered line represents a single instruction; thus the number of lines in the case of a macroinstruction equals the number of assembly-language instructions within the macroinstruction.

80

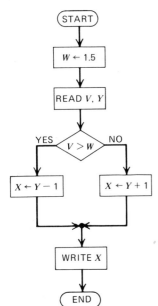

Figure 9.1. Flow chart of a program based on the statement "IF $V > W$ THEN $X \leftarrow Y - 1$ ELSE $X \leftarrow Y + 1$."

Example 9.1. In Example 3.5 (p. 14) macroinstruction MAC1 is defined as follows:

DEFINE MACRO MAC1

$\left. \begin{array}{l} \cdots \\ \cdots \\ \cdots \end{array} \right\}$ (list of the 20 instructions defining MAC1)

END

This macroinstruction is assigned 20 line numbers every time it is included in an assembly-language program.

The *labels* in Table 9.1 identify the addresses for the JUMP and GO TO instructions, and are translated into memory locations by the assembler. The *operators* are *mnemonic instruction codes* known to the assembler, the operands are variables and constants specified by the programmer, and the *comments* (usually in English or other noncomputer language) are for the information of the programmer and are ignored by the assembler.

The most commonly used assemblers are the *one-pass assembler* and the *two-pass assembler*. A one-pass assembler translates an assembly-language program into a machine-language program by scanning the former only once. Such an assembler, however, involves additional pro-

Table 9.1 A Program Based on the Statement "IF $V > W$ THEN $X \leftarrow Y - 1$ ELSE $X \leftarrow Y + 1$": Assembly-Language Program

Line Number	Label	Instruction		Comments
		Operator	Operands	
		EQUATE	W, 1.5	THE VALUE 1.5 IS ASSIGNED TO W.
1		READ	V	THE VALUE OF V IS READ FROM AN INPUT DEVICE.
2		READ	Y	THE VALUE OF Y IS READ FROM AN INPUT DEVICE.
3		LOAD	W	THE VALUE OF W IS LOADED INTO THE ACCUMULATOR.
4		SUBTRACT	V	THE VALUE OF V IS SUBTRACTED FROM THE CONTENTS OF THE ACCUMULATOR; THE RESULTING SIGN IS INDICATED BY THE SIGN FLAG.
5		JUMP ON FLAG < 0	L1	THE PROGRAM JUMPS TO LABEL L1 IF THE SIGN FLAG INDICATES NEGATIVE ACCUMULATOR CONTENTS.

6		LOAD	Y	THE VALUE OF Y IS LOADED INTO THE ACCUMULATOR.
7		ADD IMMEDIATE	1	THE NUMBER 1 IS ADDED TO THE CONTENTS OF THE ACCUMULATOR.
8		STORE	X	THE CONTENTS OF THE ACCUMULATOR ARE STORED AS X.
9		GO TO	FINISH	GO TO LABEL FINISH.
10	L1	LOAD	Y	THE VALUE OF Y IS LOADED INTO THE ACCUMULATOR.
11		SUBTRACT IMMEDIATE	1	THE NUMBER 1 IS SUBTRACTED FROM THE CONTENTS OF THE ACCUMULATOR.
12		STORE	X	THE CONTENTS OF THE ACCUMULATOR ARE STORED AS X.
13	FINISH	WRITE	X	WRITE THE VALUE OF X ON AN OUTPUT DEVICE.
		END		

gramming steps when forward referencing of a label occurs in the assembly-language program.

> **Example 9.2.** The assembly-language program shown in Table 9.1 is translated into a machine-language program by a one-pass assembler. In line 5, a forward reference to label L1 is encountered. The memory location represented by L1 (line number 10), however, is not yet known. Thus the assembler either must search and find L1 or must return to line 5 later for the insertion of the memory location represented by label L1.

The processing of labels is simpler in a two-pass assembler. Such an assembler passes (scans) through the assembly-language program twice. During the first pass it recognizes the labels and generates a *symbol table* that consists of the labels and their memory locations. The assembly-language instructions are translated into machine-language instructions during the second pass. Information generated in the first pass is often transmitted for use in the second pass via external memory such as paper tape or magnetic disk.

9.2. LOADERS

A machine-language program may be read into the main memory of the microcomputer by a *loader* program. The loader reads in the instructions sequentially and it also searches for subroutines that are requested by the program and that are already *resident* in the memory (*library routines*). Some loaders are also capable of *relocating* the program: this feature is particularly useful when two or more separate programs are loaded into the main memory.

   When starting the operation of the microcomputer, a short loader, often designated a *bootstrap loader,* is used to prepare the microcomputer for the loading of the first program (usually a larger loader) into the main memory. The bootstrap loader may be stored in a permanent memory such as hard-wired logic, read-only memory, paper tape, or magnetic disk. Alternatively, it may be read in manually via front panel controls.

9.3. DATA STRUCTURES

Data structures provide for the storage and retrieval of *related* data in a microcomputer system. Any method that permits the retrieval of such data may be considered a data structure; in what follows, however, attention is limited to *stacks* and *queues*, both of which are stored in *sequential memory locations*. Another important data structure, the *array*, is discussed briefly in Problems 3 and 4 at the end of the chapter.

Stacks

One of the simplest data structures, commonly used in subroutine linkages, is the stack, also known as *push-down stack*, or *last-in-first-out* or *LIFO stack*. In a stack all accesses are made at one end of a group of sequential memory locations. Three representations of a 7-word stack are shown in Figure 9.2. The representation in the leftmost column shows the stack as a push-down stack. (This is similar to a push-down stack of plates with spring return found in cafeterias where the top plate remains at the same level while plates are added to or removed from the stack). The upper row in Figure 9.2 shows the stack with 3 words filled, the lower row with an additional word 1111 added on top. We

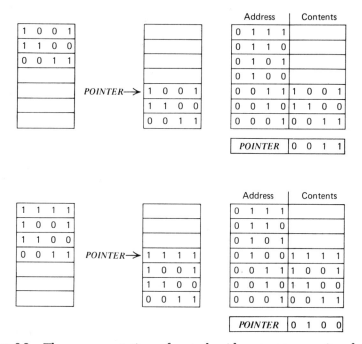

Figure 9.2. Three representations of a stack with a storage capacity of seven 4-bit words. Upper row: 3 words of the stack filled; lower row: 4 words of the stack filled.

can see that in the leftmost representation the contents of the stack are
pushed down and the new word is added on top. If a word is now removed, it is the last one that had been added previously, that is, the
word 1111, and the stack will revert to its preceding state shown in the
upper row of Figure 9.2. This representation of the stack can be directly
realized by bidirectional shift registers.

Another representation of a stack is shown in the second column of
Figure 9.2. This resembles vertically stacked books where all additions
and removals take place at the top of the stack. The height of the stack
is indicated by the *pointer*. This representation can be realized in a main
memory or in a scratch-pad memory as shown in the rightmost column of
Figure 9.2. Note that a separate address has been provided for the
storage of the pointer.

Flow charts for stack operations are shown in Figure 9.3 with reference to the rightmost representation of Figure 9.2. An add-to-stack or
push stack routine is shown in Figure 9.3*a*, a remove-from-stack or *pop
stack* routine in Figure 9.3*b*. Note that these routines make no provisions
to detect a *stack overflow* that occurs when the stack is full and the addition of a word to the stack is initiated. Similarly, there is no provision to
detect a *stack underflow* that occurs when the stack is empty and the
removal of a word is initiated. Such provisions are usually included in
larger systems; in smaller systems, however, they remain the responsibility of the programmer.

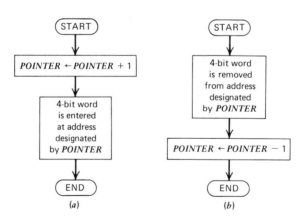

Figure 9.3. Stack routines. (*a*) Add-to-stack or "push stack." (*b*) Remove-
from-stack or "pop stack."

Queues

Another data structure, commonly used in waiting for access to input and output devices, is the waiting *queue*. All additions to a queue are made at its *tail* and all removals are made at its *head*.

Four representations of a queue are shown in Figure 9.4. The leftmost column can be realized by serial-in parallel-out shift registers. The representation of the second column is rarely used and is included only for completeness.

In the representation of the third column of Figure 9.4, the contents are not shifted. This representation can be realized in a main memory or in a scratch-pad memory as shown in the rightmost column. Note that the addition of a word and the removal of one causes the queue to move up by one location. Thus the queue would run out of memory space even when it is only partially full. This is prevented by wrapping-around, that is, by declaring address 0111 $= 7_{10}$ adjacent to address 0 as illustrated in the queue routines of Figure 9.5. These routines operate the queue properly as long as no *queue overflow* or *queue underflow* occurs. Provisions to detect overflow and underflow again remain the responsibility of the programmer in smaller systems, and are somewhat more involved than those required for stack operations.

9.4. SUBROUTINE LINKAGES

The call of a subroutine and the return from it involve several operations collected under the term *subroutine linkage*. One of these is storing in a stack the contents of the program counter to serve as a *return address*. The same stack may be also used for storing the contents of registers and flags in order to make these storage elements available for use by the subroutine. The subroutine linkage also provides for the passing of *parameters* between the main program and the subroutine.

> **Example 9.3.** This example illustrates the use of subroutine linkages and passing of parameters in a program that reads the value of x from paper tape, calls a subroutine that computes $x + \sqrt{x}$, calls a subroutine that computes $\sqrt{x}$, and prints out the result. Note that the purpose of the program is to illustrate the use of subroutine linkages, hence it is not necessarily optimal (see also Problem 5 at the end of the chapter). Also note that many of the instructions would have to be macroinstructions in a microcomputer.

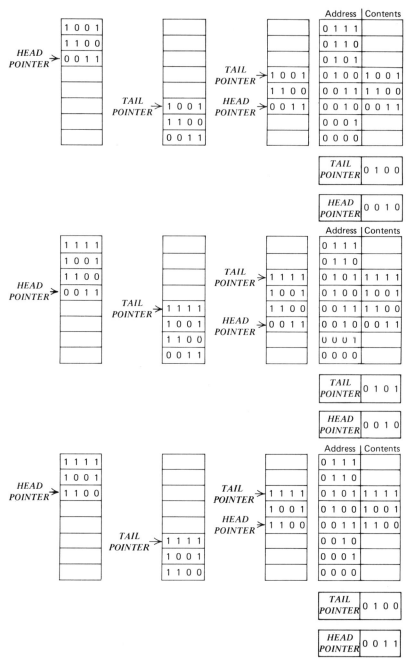

Figure 9.4. Four representations of a queue with a storage capacity of eight 4-bit words. Top row: 3 words of the queue filled; middle row: the queue of the top row with the word 1111 added; bottom row: the queue of the middle row with the word 0011 removed.

88

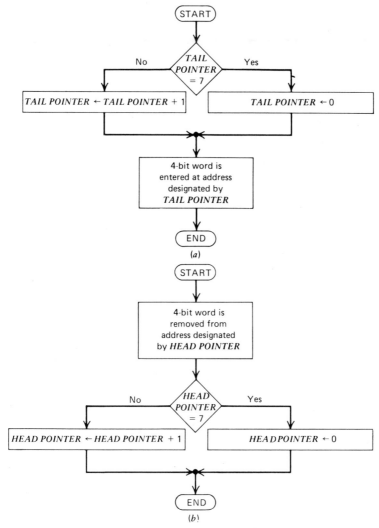

Figure 9.5. Queue routines. (*a*) Add-to-queue. (*b*) Remove-from-queue.

The program is shown in Table 9.2. It is divided into three parts that are located in three areas of the main memory: the *main program area*, the *parameter area*, and the *subroutine area*. The parameter area (often located within the base page) must be addressable both from the main program area and from the subroutine area. However, no addressing is required between

Table 9.2 Computation of $x + \sqrt{x}$: The Program

MEMORY LOCATION	CONTENTS

Main program area of memory

0	Start
1	Read paper tape and store the number in memory location 16
2	Call subroutine computing $x + \sqrt{x}$ from memory location 32
3	Print out the contents of memory location 17
4	Stop

Parameter area of memory

16	Input x to subroutine computing $x + \sqrt{x}$
17	Output of subroutine computing $x + \sqrt{x}$
18	Input to subroutine "squareroot"
19	Output of subroutine "squareroot"

Subroutine area of memory

32	Start subroutine $x + \sqrt{x}$
33	Store contents of memory location 16 in memory location 35
34	Go to memory location 36
35	Storage of the input to subroutine computing $x + \sqrt{x}$
36	Store contents of memory location 35 in memory location 18
37	Call subroutine "squareroot" from memory location 48
38	Add the contents of memory location 19 to the contents of memory location 35 and store the result in memory location 40
39	Go to memory location 41
40	Storage of $x + \sqrt{x}$
41	Store the contents of memory location 40 in memory location 17
42	Return from subroutine computing $x + \sqrt{x}$
48	Start subroutine "squareroot"
49	Store the contents of memory location 18 in memory location 51
50	Go to memory location 52
51	Storage of the input to subroutine "squareroot"
52	⎫ These three steps compute the square root of the number
53	⎬ stored in memory location 51. The result is stored in memory
54	⎭ location 56.
55	Go to memory location 57
56	Storage of the output of subroutine "squareroot"
57	Store the contents of memory location 56 in memory location 19
58	Return from subroutine "squareroot"

the main program area and the subroutine area. Figure 9.6 shows the operation of the program counter and the stack; the latter is represented as a 2-word push-down stack of the type shown in the leftmost column of Figure 9.2.

The program starts at memory location 0 with the stack empty. After the execution of the read and store instruction in location 1, the subroutine from memory location 32 is called. As a result of this call the return address, location 3, is pushed into the stack, and the program counter is changed to the location of the called subroutine, that is, to 32 (see fourth entries from left in the top row of Figure 9.6).

Now the execution of the subroutine takes place. The parameter x that was stored by the main program in location 16 is now fetched by the instruction in memory location 33 and is stored in memory location 35. In preparation of the call of subroutine "squareroot" the instruction in location 36 stores x in location 18 of the parameter area. The instruction in location 37 calls subroutine "squareroot" from location 48. As a result of this call, return address 38 is pushed into the stack, and the program counter is changed to 48 (see rightmost entries in the top row of Figure 9.6).

Subroutine "squareroot" is executed next. It is completed by the return instruction in location 58 which pops return address 38 into the program counter (see rightmost entries in the center row of Figure 9.6). Now the execution of the first subroutine resumes and proceeds until the return instruction in location 42

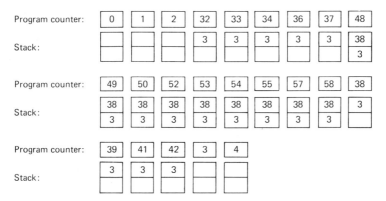

Figure 9.6. Computation of $x + \sqrt{x}$: operation of the program counter and the stack.

which pops return address 3 into the program counter. The print instruction in location 3 of the main program is executed next, and the program is terminated by the stop instruction in memory location 4.

9.5. SIMULATION

The performance of a microcomputer system should be evaluated under actual operating conditions. In many cases, however, it is also desirable to conduct a simulated test that does not require the use of external I/O devices.

> **Example 9.4.** The traffic controller microcomputer of Example 2.2. is tested in a special-purpose test setup that is controlled by a larger computer and does not include vehicle sensors or vehicles. The resulting data characterize the traffic controller for various simulated traffic conditions.

Simulation may also be used in the design of a microcomputer system. The performance of a program may be evaluated by simulating the operation of the microcomputer by means of a *simulator* program that runs on another computer.

> **Example 9.5.** A microcomputer is evaluated for use in a control system. A control program is written that meets the requirements of the control system and is in accordance with the programming rules of the microcomputer users' manual. This program and a simulator program are read into a large computer that predicts the performance of the control program and the microcomputer under actual operating conditions.

9.6. HARDWARE SHARING

Up to now it has been tacitly assumed that the microcomputer and its peripheral devices were dedicated to a single task and were executing a single program. This, however, need not always be the case. Thus an intermittently utilized peripheral device may be shared by several microcomputers.

> **Example 9.6.** Three processes in a chemical plant are controlled by three independent but adjacently located microcomputers. The programs are developed elsewhere and are available

on perforated paper tape. A program is read into the designated microcomputer via a single paper-tape reader that can be accessed by any one of the three microcomputers.

In other forms of hardware sharing, a single memory unit may be shared by several programs (*multiprogramming*) or among several microcomputers (*multiple processing*).

9.7. SYSTEM OPERATION

In addition to input and output, CPU, memory, and program, the operation of a microcomputer also requires *operating hardware* and *operating software*. Operating hardware may include front panel controls and also additional peripheral devices serving as an interface between the microcomputer and operating personnel. Operating software, often designated *operating system* or *executive program*, operates in conjunction with the operating hardware. It may include a *program editor*, or *text editor*, that facilitates changes in the program before its assembly and a *debugging routine* that operates during the execution of the program to aid in localizing errors in it. The operating system also provides sequencing of the assembler and loader operations, and it directs hardware sharing and program processing.

> **Example 9.7.** A program for a microcomputer is written in an assembly language. The result is designated a *source code* (or *source file* or *source module*) which may be a *source deck* or a *source tape*. The source code is read into the microcomputer where it is translated into machine language by the assembler. The result is an *object code* (or *object file* or *object module*) which may be an *object deck* or an *object tape*. The object code is read into the microcomputer where it is collated with referenced library routines by the *linkage editor*. The result is a *load module* that can be loaded into the main memory by a loader program.
>
> These operations are directed by the operating system and by manual intervention of operating personnel.

PROBLEMS

1. Expand the flow chart of Figure 9.3*a* to provide a stack overflow indication when the stack is full and the addition of a word to the stack is initiated.

2. Expand the flow charts of Figures 9.5a and 9.5b to provide a queue overflow indication when the queue is full and the addition of a word to the queue is initiated. Assume that initially the queue is empty and that both pointers point to location 0.

3. A widely used simple data structure that utilizes sequential memory locations is the *array*. The simplest array is a *one-dimensional array* which is an ordered list. An example of such an array is a list containing the times of the sunset for the 31 days of a month. Prepare flow charts that can store and read each *element* of this array. Include error checks that detect when access to a memory location outside the boundaries of the array (e.g., access to day 32) is initiated.

4. Extend the flow charts of Problem 3 above to a *two-dimensional array* that contains the times of the sunrise and the sunset for the 31 days of a month.

5. Consider the location of the parameter area and find a rationale for the complexity of the operations in memory locations 33 through 36 and 49 through 51 in the program of Table 9.2.

APPENDIX A   BASE-8 ARITHMETIC TABLES

Table A.1   Addition

+	1	2	3	4	5	6	7
1	2	3	4	5	6	7	10
2	3	4	5	6	7	10	11
3	4	5	6	7	10	11	12
4	5	6	7	10	11	12	13
5	6	7	10	11	12	13	14
6	7	10	11	12	13	14	15
7	10	11	12	13	14	15	16

Table A.2   Multiplication

×	1	2	3	4	5	6	7
1	1	2	3	4	5	6	7
2	2	4	6	10	12	14	16
3	3	6	11	14	17	22	25
4	4	10	14	20	24	30	34
5	5	12	17	24	31	36	43
6	6	14	22	30	36	44	52
7	7	16	25	34	43	52	61

Table A.3   Multiples of 10_{10}

BASE 10	BASE 8
10	12
20	24
30	36
40	50
50	62
60	74
70	106
80	120
90	132

APPENDIX B   BASE-16 ARITHMETIC TABLES

Table B.1   Addition

×	1	2	3	4	5	6	7	8	9	A	B	C	D	E	F	
1	2	3	4	5	6	7	8	9	A	B	C	D	E	F	10	1
2	3	4	5	6	7	8	9	A	B	C	D	E	F	10	11	2
3	4	5	6	7	8	9	A	B	C	D	E	F	10	11	12	3
4	5	6	7	8	9	A	B	C	D	E	F	10	11	12	13	4
5	6	7	8	9	A	B	C	D	E	F	10	11	12	13	14	5
6	7	8	9	A	B	C	D	E	F	10	11	12	13	14	15	6
7	8	9	A	B	C	D	E	F	10	11	12	13	14	15	16	7
8	9	A	B	C	D	E	F	10	11	12	13	14	15	16	17	8
9	A	B	C	D	E	F	10	11	12	13	14	15	16	17	18	9
A	B	C	D	E	F	10	11	12	13	14	15	16	17	18	19	A
B	C	D	E	F	10	11	12	13	14	15	16	17	18	19	1A	B
C	D	E	F	10	11	12	13	14	15	16	17	18	19	1A	1B	C
D	E	F	10	11	12	13	14	15	16	17	18	19	1A	1B	IC	D
E	F	10	11	12	13	14	15	16	17	18	19	1A	1B	1C	1D	E
F	10	11	12	13	14	15	16	17	18	19	1A	1B	1C	1D	1E	F
	1	2	3	4	5	6	7	8	9	A	B	C	D	E	F	

Table B.2   Multiplication

×	1	2	3	4	5	6	7	8	9	A	B	C	D	E	F	
1	1	2	3	4	5	6	7	8	9	A	B	C	D	E	F	1
2	2	4	6	8	A	C	E	10	12	14	16	18	1A	1C	1E	2
3	3	6	9	C	F	12	15	18	1B	1E	21	24	27	2A	2D	3
4	4	8	C	10	14	18	1C	20	24	28	2C	30	34	38	3C	4
5	5	A	F	14	19	1E	23	28	2D	32	37	3C	41	46	4B	5
6	6	C	12	18	1E	24	2A	30	36	3C	42	48	4E	54	5A	6
7	7	E	15	1C	23	2A	31	38	3F	46	4D	54	5B	62	69	7
8	8	10	18	20	28	30	38	40	48	50	58	60	68	70	78	8
9	9	12	1B	24	2D	36	3F	48	51	5A	63	6C	75	7E	87	9
A	A	14	1E	28	32	3C	46	50	5A	64	6E	78	82	8C	96	A
B	B	16	21	2C	37	42	4D	58	63	6E	79	84	8F	9A	A5	B
C	C	18	24	30	3C	48	54	60	6C	78	84	90	9C	A8	B4	C
D	D	1A	27	34	41	4E	5B	68	75	82	8F	9C	A9	B6	C3	D
E	E	1C	2A	38	46	54	62	70	7E	8C	9A	A8	B6	C4	D2	E
F	F	1E	2D	3C	4B	5A	69	78	87	96	A5	B4	C3	D2	E1	F
	1	2	3	4	5	6	7	8	9	A	B	C	D	E	F	

APPENDIX C   TABLE OF POWERS OF 2

	2^n	n	2^{-n}					
	1	0	1.0					
	2	1	0.5					
	4	2	0.25					
	8	3	0.125					
	16	4	0.0625					
	32	5	0.03125					
	64	6	0.01562	5				
	128	7	0.00781	25				
	256	8	0.00390	625				
	512	9	0.00195	3125				
	1024	10	0.00097	65625				
	2048	11	0.00048	82812	5			
	4096	12	0.00024	41406	25			
	8192	13	0.00012	20703	125			
	16384	14	0.00006	10351	5625			
	32768	15	0.00003	05175	78125			
	65536	16	0.00001	52587	89062	5		
1	31072	17	0.00000	76293	94531	25		
2	62144	18	0.00000	38146	97265	625		
5	24288	19	0.00000	19073	48632	8125		
10	48576	20	0.00000	09536	74316	40625		
20	97152	21	0.00000	04768	37158	20312	5	
41	94304	22	0.00000	02384	18579	10156	25	
83	88608	23	0.00000	01192	09289	55078	125	
167	77216	24	0.00000	00596	04644	77539	0625	
335	54432	25	0.00000	00298	02322	38769	53125	
671	08864	26	0.00000	00149	01161	19384	76562	5
1342	17728	27	0.00000	00074	50580	59692	38281	25
2684	35456	28	0.00000	00037	25290	29846	19140	625
5368	70912	29	0.00000	00018	62645	14923	09570	3125
10737	41824	30	0.00000	00009	31322	57461	54785	15625
21474	83648	31	0.00000	00004	65661	28730	77392	57812	5
42949	67296	32	0.00000	00002	32830	64365	38696	28906	25

REFERENCES

1. Barna, A. and Porat, D. I., *Integrated Circuits in Digital Electronics*, Wiley-Interscience, New York, 1973.

2. Flores, I., *Peripheral Devices*, Prentice-Hall, Inc., Englewood Cliffs, N. J., 1973.

3. Husson, S. S., *Microprogramming, Principles and Applications*, Prentice-Hall, Inc., Englewood Cliffs, N. J., 1970.

4. Knuth, D. E., *Fundamental Algorithms, The Art of Computer Programming*, Addison-Wesley Publishing Company, Reading, Mass., 1968.

5. Korn, G. A., *Minicomputers for Engineers and Scientists*, McGraw-Hill Book Company, New York, 1973.

6. Stone, H. S., *Introduction to Computer Organization and Data Structures*, McGraw-Hill Book Company, New York, 1972.

ANSWERS TO SELECTED PROBLEMS

Chapter 2

1: 39 plus ground return.

Chapter 3

1: 00000101, 00001011, 11111111. 7: 51.

Chapter 4

1: From the right to the left.

Chapter 5

1: 45, 0.71875, 6.625. 2: 1111011, 0.01001, 11100000.011.
7: 1 1001 0011.0010; 1 0001 0111.0010 0101; 1.0111 0110 1001.
9: $E = 0\ 1000$, $M = 0\ 111101$; $E = 0\ 0101$, $M = 1\ 01000101$; $E = 0\ 0100$, $M = 0\ 101000001$; $E = 1\ 1011$, $M = 1\ 01011$.

Chapter 7

1: 32. 5: $41{,}984_{10}$, $42{,}075_{10}$.

Chapter 8

2: OF_{16}, $C104B5_{16}$ (5 times), 101_{10}. 6: No, yes. 7: 8 microseconds, 5 microseconds. 8: *RECEIVE 1* = 0, *SEND 1* = 1, *RECEIVE 2* = 1, *SEND 2* = 0, *RECEIVE 3* = 1, *SEND 3* = 0.

Chapter 9

5: Minimizing the use of indirect addressing.

Index